MW01141258

WITH WINGS AS

Eagles

ANN STEWART

WITH WINGS AS EAGLES

ISBN # 1-894928-46-6

All Scripture quotations in this volume are from
the King James Version of the Bible

Printed in the United States of America

Dedication

This book is dedicated to all the ministries and individuals who held us up in prayer before the Lord Jesus Christ, who is our Healer, our Comforter, our Everpresent Help in Trouble. He is the One who came through miraculously time and time again. He is the One whom we glorify and offer our heartfelt thanks to.

Endorsement

Jack's story is a must read as it takes you inside the life of a warrior; a mighty man of God, who refused to quit. This book will build your faith and confidence in Christ as it tells the story of a family that clung to the promises of the Word, of friends who stood by, and of a man whose passion for life will inspire many.

Pastor Scott Debrecen
Living Word Community Church

Contents

Introduction

This is Jack's story; of how he lay in a hospital bed for months, not knowing who he was, where he was, or what he was. Even subsequent to his homecoming, after a series of traumatic trials, errors, physical pain and mental anguish, he was beset with a stroke, paralysis and trauma about his ordeals. But... he had a personal encounter with the Lord, who told him: "Take my hand; I'll lead you through it," and since that moment he has been living one day at a time to the fullest in his gradual recuperation over the past 4 years. Each day has been one of increasing faith, joy and healing with his focus solely fastened on the day at hand, in anticipation of what the Lord is going to do next. He has not looked back. Now he proclaims what the Lord has done to everyone he meets. He has made a conscious decision not to dwell on the horrors behind him.

The whole story must be told, and the Lord has gently prompted me to do so at this time when the emotional wounds have healed. Jack can now finally look back triumphantly at the wondrous works the Lord has done. Although Jack is the principal subject, due to short-term memory loss, medications and trauma, he "was not there." Consequently he has only been able to fill in a few blanks from his perspective.

I am so grateful to the Holy Spirit who literally let my fingers glide over the keyboard as he gave me instant recollection of all the facts. What I thought would be an endless, painful task turned out to be an assignment of love. This book has been written for the express purpose of blessing many and of letting everyone who reads it know how precious our Lord is. What he has done for Jack, he can do for you.

My greatest blessings in looking back have been to see how the Lord has carried Jack and our whole family **with wings as eagles**. Although we saw, felt, and acknowledged his Presence during the trials, this overview of everything that transpired has been an awesome revelation of the magnitude and magnificence of our God.

Jack's Prologue

It may seem strange to hear me say this, but I don't regret it. My dear wife, Ann, has described that what I went through was no piece of cake, to the point that even now I do not like looking back...but God! What I went through I would not wish on anybody. However, today I realize that I would never have had the relationship with the Lord I now enjoy if I had not gone through it. Everything that the medical profession told me I would never do, I am doing. I enjoy life, I pass every physical, and I am involved in business, even though I still have the one problem. I may have a little trouble walking, but I sure don't have any problem talking!

The question has been asked several times: "Why did you not want to stay and live in glory forever; why come back here?" Well, I'll tell you why. In fact, I get upset every time I hear it because I'm not a quitter! These are exciting times; being the end-times. I have a job to do; my mission here is not finished. I have a ministry of healing and encouragement because I have been there!

The toughest part for me was hearing over and over again what I would never be able to do. That is when in my spirit I would hear: "Whose report do you believe: theirs or mine?" That would boost my faith. The Lord "endured the cross for the joy that was put before him, despising the shame, and is set down at the right hand of the throne of God."* Do you think he looks back at the shame and agony of the cross? I heard him say clearly to me: "Where am I now, Jack? From now on it's a piece of cake!"

Jack Stewart

* Heb. 12:2

xi

1. The Onset

"*Ann, I fell down the stairs,*" *came a faint, faltering voice, almost apologetically.* "*Last thing I know I was eating a banana by the back door at the top of the stairs and suddenly boom, I'm on the bottom step with a gash on my left knee and what feels like a big bruise on my right shoulder. I crawled to the couch to recoup and get my bearings. Must have fainted, but feel better now. I'll be fine!*"

It is September 24, 1998. I am at work, early afternoon, downtown. What do I do from here? "*Do you need an ambulance,*" *I ask, knowing my hubby's aversion to hospitals.*

"*No! I'm fine now; must have been the banana I ate.*"

"*Yeah, but you never know, I'm calling the ambulance from here; at least let them check you out; if they think you need to be treated in the hospital, go, O.K, Jack?*"

"*All right, but take your time. I feel a lot better now.*"

"*I'm leaving work right now. In the meanwhile, call Sergio to see if he can come over to stay with you.*"

The next twenty-four hours disappeared in a blur. Everything went so fast. On my way out of the office I called our pastor. In the meantime Sergio, who did not have his car that day, had asked Kaz, who was close at hand, to sit with Jack.

By the time I got home Jack had refused the ambulance I had ordered. He also refused the second one that Kaz had called. Jack was in bed with a humungous headache. By the time he was rushed to the nearest hospital he was lapsing into a coma. Without adequate diagnostic equipment, the local hospital whisked Jack immediately to the Montreal General downtown.

His condition was diagnosed as an arterial leak in the centre of the medulla, the motor nerve centre of the brain. This could be either due to an aneurysm or a tear in the artery. An aneurysm, we learned, is a thinning spot in an artery which balloons into a tiny sac filled with blood. If this sac bursts, it's "lights out". The surgical procedure for this is to go in and clamp this "bubble" to keep it from leaking blood. A tear, on the other hand, cannot be "patched" and would continue filling up the brain with blood. There would be no hope.

By now it was early evening. Jack was transferred from Emergency to the Neurological Intensive Care Unit in a coma, on total life support. We would not be moved. Our two wonderful daughters Liv and Deane were standing firm with me, as were their fiancés, Sergio and Mark respectively, all praying for Jack. Along with 2 pastors and Liv's friend, Val, we were singing Praise songs to the Lord all night in the waiting area until all the diagnostic tests were completed. We know that the Bible says that:

"It is good to sing praises to our God"[1] and:

"Thou that inhabitest the praises of Israel" (his people)[2]

Now that we needed him most we did just that, and he filled us with his Peace and Reassurance. At 2 a.m., the neurosurgeon came up to tell us that the angiogram results were inconclusive. As the leak was obscured by a lot of blood, he was not able to determine exactly what it was, where, or how best to proceed. After the others left Liv, Val and I curled up as comfortably as we could in the easy chairs available.

The next morning we were told that Jack had pneumonia and a high fever. When I left home the previous morning, he seemed perfectly fine: no cough, no wheezing, no fever. The operation, we were told, would be delayed until after both the pneumonia and fever were cured. Furthermore, tests revealed that his heart was so

---

[1] Ps.147:1
[2] Ps. 22:3

bad that it might not be able to withstand any operational procedure.

The surgeon wanted to know all the circumstances surrounding Jack's previous heart attacks. I was dumbfounded. I did not know of any heart attacks! The doctor was surprised, saying that there must have been more than one judging from the condition of his heart! In my mind I tried to recall Jack's medical history.

2. Flashback

Jack was born with a heart condition referred to as a "heart murmur." At a very young age he was bedridden for over a year and told by the doctors that he would not live beyond the age of thirty, do sports of any kind, marry, or have children. On his childhood sickbed Jack remembers distinctly talking with Jesus. He just knew he was real. Although he never saw him, he somehow was aware of him; he instinctively knew that, in order to make the best of his life, he had to learn to pace himself. No doctor had ever told him that but he told me he had heard it on the inside.

As a youth Jack learned to discipline himself not to get too excited or too tired, and to do everything at a steady pace. He skated, played hockey with his friends, and spent his summers playing baseball. He did so well in baseball that he was even scouted by the St. Louis Cardinals' Major League team. However, due to lack of strength in his throwing arm, he did not "make the cut". He defied all the odds and never looked back.

By the time I got to know him at age thirty-two, he nonchalantly explained that he used to have a heart murmur but had outgrown it. When at age thirty he received the insurance settlement his parents had provided for him, he promptly repaid them by having their basement fully finished and decorated. After every medical examination he would tell me that his heart was fine. Over the years any possible heart condition was far from our minds. He passed physicals for life insurance purposes and, whenever discussing wills and life insurance, we always understood that he would be around for a long time. He was always healthy in every way; he just was not strong physically.

One afternoon the second year of our marriage Jack called me saying that he had pain all down his left arm, and that everyone in the office was telling him to go immediately to Emergency at the hospital up the street. I ran to meet him, working just a couple of blocks away, but by then he told me that he felt much better and refused to go to the hospital. Instead, he took me to a fancy restaurant where we enjoyed a long, leisurely, wonderful evening. The pain had gone completely and I knew that he was fine. At that time I had no idea of the gravity of whatever situation his heart was in, nor did I know that pain in the left arm indicated a heart problem.

Then, all of a sudden, I recalled one afternoon when Liv was 2½ years old and Deane still an infant. Jack had gone up the street to the medical centre to have a minor irritation taken care of in the doctor's office, which necessitated a shot of local anesthetic. It took him more than 2 hours to return. I remember wondering why he wasn't back yet.

When he finally came home he had a strange smile on his face, relating that when the doctor gave him the shot he had passed out. When he awoke the doctor was anxiously hovering over him, acting very quickly to give him a shot of antidote to get him back. The doctor had subsequently elaborated that he thought he had "lost" him after administering Xylocaine. He told him to carry a warning in his wallet at all times as well as to alert every doctor of his allergic reaction to this local anesthetic. At the time we were shaken a bit by it but thought no more of it over the years. I never dreamed that it was anything more serious than fainting! We had prayed about the procedure before Jack left. We knew that it was the Lord who had spared him.

At Jack's admission to the hospital I had notified the doctors of his severe allergic reaction to Xylocaine, and the neurosurgeon wanted to know exactly what type of reaction he had to it. I said that it was serious; that he had fainted and needed to be "brought back" with another shot, but that I was not present when it happened. Now, suddenly, having this sprung to memory and putting 2 and 2 together, could it be that Jack had a seizure, heart attack, or heart failure in that doctor's office? We never did see that doctor again. I praise God for having guided him in his swift

6

reaction and know-how to resuscitate my husband that day long ago! Yet, if Jack was healed then, he was healed!

Then I remembered another occasion in '89 when Jack was in hospital for tests regarding symptoms indicative of a brain tumour. I was called at work to rush to the hospital. Jack was stable now, they told me, but he had died suddenly and they had to resuscitate him. I recalled that he had actually died at that time but I never considered it a heart attack; I did not know. Now I realized that no matter what the cause of death, the heart stops! Technically, I suppose that could be construed as a heart attack, or heart failure! The point is that we had put it behind us over all those years. Jack had been happy, active, and enjoying a full life! Therefore, I was not daunted by these new revelations. If the Lord had healed him, once healed, then always healed!

The Lord further refreshed my memory that the tests back then had revealed no brain tumour, but Jack was put on strong medication which only made him feel worse. The doctors had admitted that they did not know what it was and, after observation and a myriad of more testing and drugs, we both decided that he was better off without medication at home. One morning a couple of weeks after his homecoming I got a call at work. "Hi", he said in a clear voice: "I am healed!" Before he could even get the words out I knew that he was totally healed just from his joyful voice! He said that from his bed, still with his eyes closed, it was as if he saw an invisible arm at the door beckoning him into the hall. He got up and, as he entered the hallway, the pressure and confusion in his brain totally left – instantly! Wow! Thank you, Lord!

These sudden insights came over a couple of days in my quiet time with the Lord. It never came up again with the doctor; so I never told him. Jack had been healed, he was healed, and now he was going to be healed again.

3. Periphery

Jack remained in a coma until 1 a.m. the following day. The nurse came into the waiting room to announce the good news, as she had promised. We had been hoping and expecting it as some subtle signs had been indicative that he was slowly coming out of it. We celebrated by running into the I.C.U. to "talk" to Dad, encouraging him to hang in there. To the eye there was no difference except that he moved a little and could, barely, move his finger on command.

The following morning the doctor explained that now that Jack was out of the coma they would have to put him into a medically induced coma in order to keep his head perfectly immobile for the blood in the brain to drain out. They had inserted a tiny pipe into the cranium at the back of the head to this effect, which had to remain perfectly horizontal to drain into a calibrated cylinder measuring every drop.

Val, Liv's best friend, and whom we considered as our third daughter, was a valuable source of medical information. What she did not know, she made it her business to find out. She was very fond of Jack, who had been like a father to her, often including her in father-daughter outings, like baseball games, etc. Val at that time was a medical secretary at another hospital just down the street. She had taken a couple of days off, her bosses being very sympathetic about the situation.

To the right of Jack's bed, from our view facing him, lay a man of around fifty. He slept a lot, but seemed sound otherwise, i.e. no coma, no major hookups. It turned out that he had an inoperable brain tumour. He was released after about a week. We got to know his wife, who would walk up and down the 7 flights of stairs two or three times a day! She was such an encouragement to me to keep as fit as possible, even though everything within me was physically depleted! And she, in turn, kept telling me how she was awed by our faith, and marveled at the stream of friends who kept coming to pray and/or sing with Jack.

By the second day it suddenly hit me: "I've been here before; same bed, same I.C.U.!" My thoughts went back a few years when I went to pray for my friend Lynette's father, who had a sudden massive stroke. An active member of our Full Gospel Chapter, he was much loved and has since been sorely missed.

The I.C.U. environment felt like a dark abyss. It had no windows; death stared you in the face from every bed, and praying in that milieu was next to impossible. Dealing with the fact that your own loved one was on the brink of death was traumatic enough, but you could not help being caught up with the traumas the families of other patients were going through. Some felt the need to share with someone going through similar trials; others needed a touch, a prayer.

The third night we were not alone in the fourteenth floor waiting room. We shared it with a French Canadian family from Sherbrooke, Quebec. They shared with us that their relative, a young man in his early thirties, lying in a coma to our left of Jack, had been hit on the back of the head with a heavy, blunt object. There were no clues, no suspects but, as it had been declared a murder case, he had to be kept on a respirator until it stopped. Three days in a row they got calls to come as his death was imminent. Each time they had to make the 2-hour trek and back, before the respirator finally stopped and he was officially declared dead by the coroner. It was heartbreaking for them.

That same night, as all the above unfolded, a young lady and her mother came charging through, crying. A young man of around eighteen had arrived a couple of days earlier. He was in a coma with most of his head bandaged; yet his legs were constantly moving in a bicycling motion. While biking to work one morning, a truck door had swung open just as he came alongside the parked vehicle, knocking him down. He had no identification on him and television ads with his picture cried out for someone to identify him. His sister had seen the announcement, but did not recognize him. Two days later, having had no contact from him, it hit her that the bandaged person on T.V. could be her brother. Much praying went on for him, and we shared the love of God and his healing power with his family.

In the meantime, our church family and many others came in a steady stream sitting and praying with Jack. They were wonderful, tangible support. Several evangelistic ministries were also praying for Jack. The news spread quickly far and wide. Despite the horrible circumstances and seemingly insurmountable trials bombarding us, we felt undergirded and truly came to understand the scriptures:

> *"The Peace of God, which passeth all understanding, shall keep your hearts and minds through Christ Jesus"*[3]

and

> *"They that wait upon the LORD shall renew their strength; they shall mount up **with wings as eagles**;"*[4]

---

[3] Phil. 4:7
[4] Isa. 40:31

4. Preparation

On the fourth day a doctor explained that they had to perform a tracheotomy, a tube inserted through a hole pierced through the base of the neck, which would be attached to the respirator. They explained that it was hospital protocol to do this with every patient who would be on a respirator for more than a week. We cringed, especially when we heard that after prolonged use the vocal chords could be adversely affected! No one who knows Jack could imagine him not being able to talk! He is a communicator! You can take almost anything from him, but not his voice!

Two gentlemen had come early one morning and prayed so loudly and fervently over Jack that literally all the alarms on the life support systems had gone off! How I wish I had been there! We were admonished by the head nurse to never allow these two gentlemen back in I.C.U.! If only she knew! Knowing right away who they were, and their fervor for the Lord, we could hardly contain our delight! I knew without any hint of doubt that something had been broken in the spirit; that Jack was healed! No, he still looked the same: the pneumonia had not totally gone yet, and there were even more complications.

A lot of the medical jargon went in one ear and out the other. Yes, they did try to transliterate as much as possible in laymen's terminology and Val explained a lot, which was helpful, but... we did not want to listen to the bad news. We kept hoping and looking forward to the healing! On that weekend I noticed on the bulletin board that another doctor was on duty. We did not get to meet her. There were so many doctors, residents and other medical personnel coming and going that it was hard to figure out who was who unless they introduced themselves.

On Monday morning I was told that they would operate the next day. I was excited and asked if I could speak with the surgeon. They informed me that it would be the doctor who had been on duty during the weekend. We had come to know Jack's neurosurgeon so well; he had gone out of his way to explain everything to us in layman's language and we had confidence in him. Being both neurosurgeon and teacher, he was reportedly in demand around the world. He was on the McGill University Health Centre teaching staff, on assignment at the Montreal General Hospital. He had been there from the moment Jack was admitted, and we considered him to be the one the Lord had put in charge of Jack's case.

What to do now! We still had not met this other doctor, and she was not available at that time. However, they promised to ask her to stop by and speak to us later that day. I prayed for wisdom. It occurred to me that I certainly had a say in the decision of which surgeon would operate on Jack. I asked the resident if he could page our neurosurgeon and ask if he would be available to perform the operation. Although he was out of town, he accepted instantly, and would be in that evening to speak with us. We all felt a sense of relief.

After supper the resident doctor explained all the consequences that could result from the operation, i.e. major paralyses of all parts of the body, including blindness, deafness, and death. The site was in the medulla, which sends nerve impulses all over the body. As this scenario was unfolding at Jack's bedside, I was keenly aware that he could hear everything, even though he was still in an induced coma. Words can bless or curse, even when spoken outside a person's hearing range. I told the doctor that I understood all the negative possibilities, but that we were Christians and believed in a positive outcome. I said it loudly to make sure Jack heard that. According to the Bible, fear is the opposite of faith and we wanted Jack to be expecting his healing along with all of us.

When the neurosurgeon arrived with his team, he also went over some of the negative implications and answered some questions that arose, gesturing with his hands as he described the procedure. I reached over, cupped his hands in mine, looked him straight in the eye, and said: "These hands are anointed. We have prayed that God would use them and guide them, and that he would give you wisdom during the operation." He silently nodded in acknowledgement, staring at his hands. It was time to sign the waiver, releasing the hospital from any of those possible consequences. He subsequently showed us on the large diagram of the brain on the wall exactly where he calculated the leak to be. Up until now it had been completely obscured by the clotted blood and they could not be sure of its exact location.

5. The Agony

Jack was taken to the operating room at 8:30 the next morning, and I was told he'd be back by noon. Liv had taken the day off. We were quietly praying in the alcove facing the elevators.

An elderly lady sat down beside us. She was exhausted after going through a battery of tests that day and told us she was waiting for her daughter, "a beautiful Black nurse on the Neurosurgery floor." We engaged in animated discussion and I prayed for her medical condition. I had not met, or even noticed, any of the nurses on the floor as I usually high-tailed it past there straight to I.C.U. at the far end of the long corridor. The nurse in question, Sylvia, I was to find out later, had developed a strong emotional and spiritual bond with this Caucasian lady. They worshipped at the same church and Sylvia had "adopted" her, her own mother being in Jamaica.

Ten minutes to 6! The elevator doors swung open and there was Jack. Well... what I could see of him. They whisked him right through and told us that we would not be able to see him for at least half an hour while they did all the re-"hooking", monitoring his vital signs, etc. Finally, the doctor came into view, looking exhausted. He headed right towards us. "I couldn't get it", he said apologetically. "I just couldn't see it. I cleaned out most of the blood clots but I just could not see it!" In shock I thanked him for his meticulous work. He had done the best he could.

I was stunned; numb. So was Liv. She turned white..."Liv, Liv??" Down she went, instantly on the floor. She had fainted. An orderly immediately got her settled on a bed in one of the rooms. It had been a long day. Time to go home! The main thing was that Jack was fine; all his vital signs were good considering the circumstances, and it seemed that there was no major nerve damage.

"What now," I asked the surgeon the next morning, "you can't operate a second time, can you?" "At least not until the scar is completely healed!" The doctor shook his head. "There is another procedure," he said somewhat hesitantly, "but it cannot be done in this hospital. Jack would have to be transported by ambulance to another hospital, which had a team of pioneers in the field of angiogram radiology. He described that in this procedure a miniscule camera would be inserted into the artery through the groin and up to the aneurysm. Subsequently, a tiny metal loop would be tightened around the oozing bulge on the artery, thereby sealing it.

In the meantime we were all still assuming and hoping that it was indeed an aneurysm; they were as yet none the wiser. It is marvelous what medical science can do! I was constantly amazed at all the intricate equipment and the vast knowledge of the medical staff. I was enormously thankful every day for the life support systems, worth thousands of dollars per day, that were keeping Jack alive throughout all delays of this ordeal.

6. Abiding

"Lord, what is this all about?" I told him how I had been expecting a miraculous healing for` Jack, and had actually envisioned him sitting right up in bed, totally healed! Was the Lord going to heal him through a miracle? Did he not want to use doctors? Did he, after 8½ hours of cracking the skull and probing inside, not want the doctor to touch the exact spot? Would it have ruptured during the process? Did he, who had guided the doctor's hands, allow only the cleaning but not the touching? After all, we had prayed specifically for his guidance and wisdom.

That night, exhausted, I fell to my knees and asked God to forgive me for any doubt in my heart. It is easy to stand in perfect faith when you're alone at home or in a prayer group. However, when you're in the thick of the battle, seeing your loved one's condition, the doctor's frowns, and the constant monitoring of a life-and-death situation, it is very hard not to despair from time to time.

The whole ordeal had taken a toll on me both emotionally and physically. I confessed any lack of faith on my part and resolved that, no matter what the circumstances looked like or what the doctors predicted, I would look to his truth, which states simply:

"He that dwelleth in the secret place of the most High shall abide under the shadow of the Almighty,"[5]

"I am the Lord that Healeth thee,"[6] and

---

[5] Ps. 91:1
[6] Ex. 15:26

"He shall call upon me, and I will answer him; I will be with him in trouble; I will deliver him, and honour him...with long life will I satisfy him, and show him my salvation"[7].

I stood on those three scriptures, speaking them over him every day. The word salvation, coming from the Greek word "Sozo" also means "healing" and "deliverance". I was blessed that we did not have to rely on our faith alone. We were covered with prayer from an army of faith-filled brothers and sisters in Christ. The Word of God says that after "having done all, stand!"[8] In other words, The Lord heard our prayer the very first time; we just had to wait in expectation for the result to manifest itself.

A peace came over me and I thanked him over and over again for his goodness, his love, his presence, his peace, and all that he is. I thanked him that Jack had come through the operation without any further complications, and reaffirmed Jack's healing, telling him that, however he was going to do it, and no matter what the outcome, he would get the glory.

"It is a good thing to give thanks unto the Lord, and to sing praises unto thy name, O most High. To show forth thy lovingkindness in the morning, and thy faithfulness every night".[9]

My favourite place to pray was on Mount Royal. The hospital is built into the mountain; its main entrance on the 6th floor faces the mountain across the street, and its back entrance on the first floor overlooks the city. Those beautiful autumn days I would just cross Cedar Ave. and climb right up a winding path to a little knoll I had discovered with a spectacular panorama. It looked out right over top of the hospital onto parts of the city below, astride the mighty St. Lawrence River and the South Shore beyond. It was a

---

[7] Ps. 91:15,16
[8] Eph. 6:13
[9] Ps. 92:1,2

place where I could unwind, take some deep breaths, read the Word, pray, and nestle under his wings.

7. Up Against the Mountain

Every day I was conscious of the fact that I had a new day to seek the Lord earnestly and to pray, in case I had missed it somehow the previous day. We had both been born-again Spirit-filled Christians for about twenty years and had seen and received miraculous healings in the past, but we never had to stand for any healing like this one!

We were literally experiencing a "hands-on healing-in-the-making" season in our lives. It basically entails having child-like faith, knowing that the bible says that:

"And this is the confidence that we have in him, that if we ask any thing according to his will, he heareth us; and if we know that he hear us, whatsoever we ask, we know that we have the petitions that we desired of him."[10]

Sounds too simple? But that is what God says. We believe it, and that settles it! It's that simple. However, if we don't know him as our personal Lord and Saviour and we don't know His Word, then we cannot stand in faith, not knowing what the Word has to say about it.

"Faith cometh by hearing, and hearing by the word of God"[11]

Furthermore,

---

[10] 1 John 5:14-15
[11] Rom.10:17

"...without faith it is impossible to please him (God); for he that cometh to God must believe that he is, and that he is a rewarder of them that diligently seek him"[12]

and

"...faith is the substance of things hoped for, the evidence of things not seen."[13]

It is this latter scripture in Hebrews that puzzles a lot of people. After all, you see that the man is dying! Without life support he would not be here! You hear what the doctors say! How can you then say that he is healed!?? I'll tell you why.

In the book of 1 Peter we see:

*"...by whose stripes you **were** healed,"*[14]

Here Peter was quoting Isaiah, who prophesied about the Messiah coming and dying on the cross for us about 700 years B.C., stating then in the present tense that:

*"...he hath borne our griefs (sickness), and carried our sorrows: yet we did esteem him stricken, smitten of God, and afflicted. But he was wounded for our transgressions, he was bruised for our iniquities; the chastisement of our peace was upon him; and with his stripes we **are** healed."*[15]

The Word of God, here prophesied through Isaiah, was already on the earth. It meant that God said it, and it would come to pass. In fact, anyone who believed that Word back then before the Messiah ever arrived would be healed, as will anyone right now who believes Him. You see, God says:

---

[12] Heb. 11:6
[13] Heb. 11:1
[14] 1 Pet. 2:24
[15] Heb. 11:6

"...my word shall not return unto me void, but it shall accomplish that which I please, and it shall prosper in the thing whereto I sent it"[16]

After all,

"Jesus Christ the same yesterday, and today, and forever."[17]

He doesn't say one thing in one chapter and something altogether opposite somewhere else. He cannot lie. He is The Truth:

"God is not a man, that he should lie; neither the son of man, that he should repent: hath he said, and shall he not do it? Or hath he spoken, and shall he not make it good?"[18]

I know that indeed we are not to deny the facts, i.e. what we see and what the doctors tell us. But, then there is the Truth! That is what God has to say about it! No matter what the factual reality is, the spiritual truth will always overcome the physical, no matter how dismal it looks; as long as there is faith connected to it!

We are emotional beings living in a physical body. When we are "born again," by asking Jesus Christ to become Lord over our lives, our spirit is infused with the Holy Spirit, hence re-born. The physical and emotional parts of us are subject to this world, which, through Adam and Eve, is ruled by the prince of this world, Satan.[19] But:

"...whatsoever is born of God overcometh the world; and this is the victory that overcometh the world, even our

---

[16] Isa. 55:11
[17] Heb. 13:8
[18] Num. 23:19
[19] John 12:31

*faith. Who is he that overcometh the world, but he that
believeth that Jesus is the Son of God?* "[20]

O.K., so here I am, constantly talking to God about what I
know he says in his Word, and reminding Him that:

*"...whosoever shall say unto this mountain [any obstacle
in life], be thou removed, and be thou cast into the sea;
and shall not doubt in his heart, but shall believe that
those things which he says shall come to pass; he shall
have whatsoever he says. Therefore I say unto you, what
things soever you desire, when you pray, believe that you
receive them, and you shall have them. And when you
stand praying, forgive, if you have ought against any; that
your Father ...may forgive you your trespasses.* "[21]

"Well", I said to him: "I am that 'whosoever' you're talking
about, Lord. I have forgiven everyone I can think of. Please remind
me if there is anyone or anything yet that I have forgotten about; I
want to be pure before you, and don't want to let any blockage
hamper Jack's healing."

I then went about telling the "mountain," i.e. the aneurysm, to
be removed in the name of Jesus, as well as other mountains that
kept cropping up. I kept saying out loud that Jack was healed, that
his mind was sound, that his body was whole, and that the Lord
had promised him long life, quoting the verse from Psalm 91.

Jack would be sixty-five that December which, according to
the Bible, is not long life!

*"The days of our years are threescore years and ten
(seventy); and if by reason of strength they be fourscore
(eighty) years..."* [22]

---

[20] 1 John 5:4-5
[21] Mark 11:23-25
[22] Ps. 90:10

I also told the Lord that I would like to see Jack face to face and be able to talk to him, like the patriarch of old did. Israel knew when it was time for him to go; he called his twelve sons to him, gave them each a blessing, and then lay down and died![23] I knew that it is not God's wish that his children go the way Jack was, i.e. still in an induced coma and gravely ill.

---

[23] Gen. 48:49

8. A Sense of Loss

That evening, after signing for the following day's angiogram procedure and trying hard not to be affected by the possible negative results, I was talking to my best friend, Georgie, who had been battling liver cancer. I had not seen her for a while due to the intense chemotherapy regime she had to undergo, and now she was staying with her sister. Instantly I understood this to mean that the end was near. She expressed how much she would love to see me.

My heart sank. Her two adult sons had been looking after her; one had come from England to stay with her that whole last year. Tears came to my eyes as I had to tell her that my Jack, too, was at death's door and that I felt riveted to the hospital; I just had to be there with him. As Liv, Val and I were car-pooling, I did not have the car, and my personal emotional and physical fuel gauge registered on empty. The timing was just the worst imaginable. Jack and I had been praying so much for Georgie.

Georgie told me that she was in perfect peace. I could tell by her voice that she was not sure she would still be there in the morning. We tearfully said our "au revoirs" in the knowledge that we would see each other again on the other side! I was able to celebrate her life in a beautiful funeral service several days later. She was much loved and is still sorely missed.

9. Breakthrough

I had to go back to work the next morning; the very day Jack had the angiogram. I had tried to postpone my return to work, but they insisted that all my holidays and sick-leaves had been used up. First, I saw Jack off. My favourite nurse went in the ambulance with him, and I felt confident that he was in good hands, both earthly and heavenly. On the subway to work I rationalized that I was better off being busy. After all, there was nothing else to do. It was strange sitting behind my desk, swamped with work and a load of stress on my shoulders, as was the norm in that job. Thanks to my supervisor, who took my circumstances into consideration, I was allowed to leave early.

Jack had just returned when I got there and his doctor came over with a big smile on his face. "They looped it," he said. "Yes, it was a perfect aneurysm, come and see." He pointed to several enlarged X-ray photographs showing different facets of the aneurysm with the tiny loop around it. He kept saying over and over again: "I was right there! I was right there! How could I have missed it? I was at the exact spot!" Then he told me that it was a miracle that Jack had survived it without complications due to the very high risk associated with it. All that day I was in perfect peace and knew that Jack would pass through it! That truly had to be the Lord! Jack had not only survived it but, as far as they could see, there was no major damage, i.e. paralysis. Praise the Lord!

I was totally exhausted. Balancing work and hospital proved too much for me under the circumstances. This time I was the one to faint! On the advice of the doctor present I took time off to see my general practitioner regarding my own state of health. He immediately wrote a note to keep me off work for a month, to be followed up on a month-by-month basis.[i]

My job as secretary in the Department of Youth Protection was a pressure-cooker situation. There had been a lot of lay-offs (being in the same government cutback category as the medical field) and those social workers that were left had to take up the slack of the ones that had been dismissed. They would finish writing their reports at the last minute and then the onus would be on the secretaries to get it done by the deadline. Almost on a monthly basis there was someone, i.e. manager, social worker or secretary, who was on extended stress leave. It had become almost impossible to cope, even without the added stress in one's private life. Part-time or flextime were non-negotiable. I was thankful for the reprieve.

Wilf arrived the next day. Jack's brother, eight years his junior, had been kept abreast of the situation from his home in Toronto, and wanted to be there after the angiogram procedure. It was sooooo good to see him. It was an occasion for the whole extended family to gather together and celebrate. He also got to see the X-rays and chat with the doctor.

We felt that the worse was over for Jack and that we were merely waiting for a gradual recovery from now on. The reality hit home when we were told the following day that, even though the loop was around the aneurysm, it would have to be adjusted in the future. There was still some leakage. This meant that a shunt would need to be implanted. This was a long, thin tube which, attached to a valve placed in the base of the skull, was threaded just under the skin of the neck and down where it drained into the pelvic area. Once the temporary shunt would be removed, Jack could finally get off the medication that had kept him comatose!

As soon as he came back from this procedure we were told that he was going "on the floor." I was shocked. Yes, it was a good sign ...but was he ready? I still could not meaningfully communicate with him and he was still hooked up to everything! All at once he came off the respirator, the hole in his neck was patched, and his intravenous line was detached. As he was not able to swallow yet, a tube was inserted through his nose into the stomach for more solid food. It all came so suddenly! We were happy and concerned at the same time. One day comatose; the next on the floor! Even the head nurse was concerned about the lack of close monitoring on the floor due to the cutbacks that had been going on. No matter! He had been in I.C.U. exactly one month and was ready for the new phase: recuperation.

10. Recuperation

Jack was placed in a 4-man room right opposite the nurses' station. I felt relieved about that and, lo and behold, who was his bed neighbour, but our cyclist friend! We had not seen much of the family since he had left I.C.U. a couple of weeks earlier. He had most of his faculties back but, due to a severe concussion, he still had trouble communicating and was unable to walk on his own, or get up by himself. He was transferred out to rehab the next day. I was so happy; it had taken a great toll on them.

I became more and more aware of the fact that the staff on the Neurosurgery floor just did not have enough eyes and hands to go around. If I did not come in by a certain time in the morning, the orderlies would be gone and I'd learn that they did not have time to get Jack out of bed and into an easy chair for half an hour or so. This was so important for his blood circulation, even though Jack did not like it. The orderlies were there only for a certain period of time and what was not done would just have to wait for the next day. As long as I was there in time, I made sure that Jack did not miss out. I noticed that an elderly gentleman across the room, who could not feed himself, would get his full tray picked up after the meals without anyone even bothering to check whether he had touched it!

Off and on I would notice that Jack's nose-feed had clogged up. Sometimes an air bubble would get in the way and I would have to find a nurse or orderly to fix it. If left unnoticed, the patient could be without food for hours. Every now and then Jack would inadvertently pull the whole tube out of his nose during his sleep at night! I'm sure it must have been very uncomfortable. It was a whole production to get it back in. First, a technician would be called to re-install it; then a portable X-ray machine had to be summoned. It would take up to 2 hours to get the results back confirming whether or not the end of the tube was inside the stomach. If it was not in the right place, the whole procedure would have to be repeated again. This could lapse into the next day, depending on what time of day it was and/or the availability of the technicians.

In the meantime our Jack was not getting fat! He had lost a lot of weight on the intravenous fluids in I.C.U. and now this "mush." His small-boned 5'10" frame of 185 lbs. had dwindled away to skin and bones, and his "contentment" tummy was completely gone. He had received so many X-rays and scans since his arrival in the hospital that I referred to him as 'radioactive Jack.' It wasn't funny. I was very concerned about all this but it could not be helped. I just kept on praying that any negative effects of the medication and radiation would not harm him.

We continued our one-sided communication. Jack was more and more alert as to what was going on around him but still could not talk. We were anxious to see his throat healed so we could have normal conversations again. I remember standing over his bed asking him for forgiveness for the many times over the years that I had interrupted and told him that it was O.K. to be quiet for a minute in order to give others a chance to talk! We used to kid him as he was literally a waterfall of words. He was never at a loss for words: always up on the latest in sports and politics, and especially loved talking about his favourite subject: the Lord. Furthermore, I promised that I would never interrupt him again![ii]

The television was connected so he could watch CNN and get some input as to what was happening in the outside world. He did not seem interested, but I knew that the news would penetrate regardless of his lack of enthusiasm. Praise tapes now played softly as well, which had not been possible in I.C.U.

Time went by very slowly. Seemingly every day was the same. Our man was getting more and more extensive physiotherapy. The therapist had started very minor bed exercises in I.C.U. and this had steadily progressed to sitting with the legs over the side of the bed. He was amazing and Jack responded very well to him. There had been some nerve damage along the left side and the doctors suspected that there was some long-term memory loss, which was very common in aneurysm and stroke victims.

Around this time I resumed editing a book written by a McGill University professor. It was very technical with lots of painstaking diagrams and tables that had to be converted from one wordprocessing program to another. Trouble was, some parts just did not seem to want to be converted and there were a lot of glitches to be overcome. How I did this up 'til late at night for months only had to be the Lord. I know that I was resting on his Strength, Peace and Wisdom. She would drop by the hospital every now and then to exchange what I had finished with more. We had become good friends, and she got to know Jack in the process, as well as Jesus as her Lord and Saviour!

11. Stepping Up to the Plate

Jack's sixty-fifth birthday was December 4th, and it was a celebration! That evening we all gathered together with some great friends, who had been steadily holding us up in prayer, including the two-some that caused the I.C.U. bells and whistles to blow! That very day Jack was finally released from his nose feed, but was not yet allowed to drink or eat until the next day when he would start very gradually under the supervision of a therapist.

We were granted the use of the boardroom behind the nurses' station for the occasion. The girls did a great job decorating, and brought goodies and soft drinks. To our delight Jack asked for ginger ale with his face all lit up. He could only whisper a few words, but this was the first day that he showed excitement. He was so frustrated when told he could not yet have anything to drink; but after a while we gave in, giving him a few sips at a time, which he thoroughly enjoyed!

The reintroduction of food was no simple matter. He could not tolerate any solid food. It all came out almost as fast as it went in! The doctors were baffled after 2 weeks of this to the point that an endoscopy was ordered. I was allowed to peek through the scope (a tiny camera) lowered into the stomach. There was nothing physically wrong in the digestive system. I then started bringing in fresh ginger for Jack to smell immediately after each bite in an attempt to ward off nausea, as he did not tolerate Gravol. I also fortified him with vitamins. It did help a bit but the nausea continued. Then I got real mad!

A sudden realization hit my spirit that the devil wanted Jack not only incapable of speech but he wanted to do away with him, one way or another! Even though Jack had survived all odds so far, it was like an unrelenting battle! I got into real warfare coming against this spirit of death hovering over Jack in the mighty Name of Jesus, and had the whole church praying with me on this issue. I kept speaking the Word over him, saying that Jack was bought with the Blood of Jesus, and that no devil was going to do him in. This was nothing less than satanic! As a matter of fact, it became evident, not only to me but to many others, that indeed the Lord has much, much more for Jack to do here on earth and, therefore, the devil wanted to shut him up! Very, very gradually the nausea subsided.

Jack was slowly progressing. He now went to the Physiotherapy Department every morning. After more than 2 months bedridden with hardly any movement in the legs, the muscles had become very weak. They had to be carefully and very gradually brought back to strength with specific exercises. His arms also had not been used and he had to start with basic hand-eye coordination exercises.

The left arm and leg were less responsive to the workouts. Being right-handed, the left hand was not so important but the left leg was a deterrent to his learning to walk. There was no paralysis and no pain; the nerves seemed to have been slightly affected by one or both procedures. Furthermore, Jack's own motivation to succeed was not quite there yet. He seemed to be totally exhausted; every little bit was an extreme effort. This could have been related to multiple factors, i.e. the prolonged bed rest, the weakness of his heart, and a type of depression that accompanies short-term memory loss. The doctors did not have the answers. I was there every morning to encourage him, but the progress went at a snail's pace.

12. A Bride to Be

Now that Dad's condition was not critical any more, all our thoughts were redirected on issues at hand before the mishap. Liv woke up one Saturday morning, exclaiming, "Mom, we've got to find a reception hall for my wedding!" She and her fiancé, Sergio, had been planning a May 1999 wedding and her dad had been in the process of looking for a hall. They had their minds set to be married on the Saturday of Victoria Day weekend but, being a very popular long weekend in Spring, most halls were booked well in advance. Now, several months later, what were we going to do!

Liv had grabbed a small local directory off the shelf and started leafing through it. It literally fell open on a page displaying a beautiful spot with a fountain spouting from the midst of a lake. It looked gorgeous and turned out to be a golf course just off the island of Montreal that also catered to wedding receptions. "O.K., let's go and see!" The boys were notified and Mark's immediate comment was: "Maybe they'll give us a good deal if we like it and tell them we want our wedding there, too!"

Deane and Mark had been going together for over a year and a half and had already approached us a couple of times about their wish to get married. However, they were still young, even though they both were mature and conscientious for their age. They would turn nineteen and twenty respectively that coming January. Anyway, this was Liv's wedding. Liv, being the romantic type, knew exactly to the minutest detail what she wanted and what colours.

To make a long story short, we all loved the place as well as their gourmet chef facilities, and made arrangements to meet with the manager on the Monday, as he was not available that weekend. The date had been tentatively booked for a golf dinner and dance but it had not yet been confirmed with a deposit. The manager explained that the party had been given a final date for the deposit, which was on that very weekend and, since they had not made one, we got the hall! The Lord really went ahead of us to prepare that! It was a paradise for wedding photographs: spring blossoms, a lake and a fountain all at the same location.

The following Saturday morning was spent shopping for the gown. We agreed to go to St-Hubert Street in the middle of Montreal's garment district, noted for their selection, expertise and great prices. Besides, we were already familiar with the area since the girls had found their prom attire there. It did not take Liv long to find her dream gown. She picked out a perfectly matching tiara and veil, and voilà, Liv's fantasy wedding was underway! Praise the Lord! Everything just fell into place.

13. Our Family

Christmas came and went with very little noticeable change in Jack's progress, but every little nuance of transformation was a blessing. His eating very gradually improved and he narrowly missed getting his nose-feed re-implanted! On the afternoon of Christmas Eve a hospital choir, directed by a doctor, sang carols and passed out goodies and little gifts to each and every patient. They sounded very professional. It was evident that they had sacrificed time in their busy schedule to practice, and the atmosphere was very festive and joyful.

Christmas day was spent with Dad. That evening we all got together, and together made an effort to keep up the tradition as much as possible. Everyone pitched in and I was so thankful for so many expert cooks in the family. What a wonderful blessing! Liv and I both considered cooking as a necessary, important duty, whereas Deane just simply enjoyed it. She is one of those special people who can produce an elegant, nutritious meal out of very ordinary basic ingredients. In the past several years, while I was working downtown and coming home exhausted after 6 via 2 buses and the subway, she would often have a delicious dish on the table ready for us to feast on. Mark has a similar passion for cooking, when he's not busy. And Sergio: now he's a chef! No, not as a career; it just comes naturally. Just put him in a kitchen and he's in charge, totally. Out comes a gourmet meal fit for a king!

Sergio had come to Montreal with his older brother and parents at the age of 4 from Uruguay. His father had passed away a couple of years before he met Liv. His father's sudden death due to a heart attack left him with many unresolved issues. He was still in need of healing, and he instantly embraced Jack as his spiritual mentor and substitute father, to which Jack had responded eagerly.

43

A couple of years earlier Jack was given a prophetic word from the Lord in church saying that there would be a young man in his life whom he would mentor. We both knew instinctively when Sergio came into the picture that this was he! Having known the Lord as a youth, he had turned away from him in his teens.

Mark and Sergio had a common bond of martial arts and weight training. Sergio had recently rededicated his life to the Lord and was hungry for everything the Lord wanted to give him. Mark had also just received Jesus as his Lord and Saviour. Both men went about telling all their old friends about Jesus and how he had changed them, and invited them to our church!

It's really amazing to see how the Lord works; how he transforms, changes, and confirms people and situations. Sergio really bonded with Jack to the point that Liv would sometimes teasingly ask him whether he had come over to see her or her dad! She was in her final year of university at the time and had to do a lot of studying and research, so there was plenty of time for father-son bonding as well. Sergio has a son, Dillon, then 3 years old and living with his mom, but father and son saw each other on a regular basis.

Mark, a college student at the time, expressed a desire to be in business, as his dad. He insisted that he had learned more business administration from his father while working part-time with him over the years than he would learn in university. The two sets of parents got together with Deane and him to discuss the situation. We saw his ardour and desire to make Deane his wife and provide for her. We also got to know him as a very bright, serious young man with a mature head on his shoulders. Sure, he would go through the school of hard knocks, but we all knew that whatever he would set his hands to would somehow turn to gold. He had the drive, the vision and the backup of his business father. Deane had taken some time off after high school to work before entering a career in esthetics.

14. Parking Woes

I had some favourite spots to park around the hospital. Parking was difficult; there were meters, spots where you could only park for 2 hours, and others where you would have to switch at a certain time of day. So I would always aim for the spots where I could park uninterruptedly from 9 a.m. to 4 p.m. The third day of January 1999 I was blessed to park in one of those favourite spots on Cedar Ave. It was about ten minutes to 4; I was on my way home in a blustering snowstorm, but ... where was the car? As I approached the spot, it was empty! Besides, the car must have been moved only a minute or so earlier as the falling snow had not yet covered its outline! Walking back and forth, I hoped against all hopes that my memory this time was not serving me right. But there it was; the exact spot, totally empty! I called 911.

Four o'clock in January in Montreal in a snowstorm signals the start of a very congested rush hour at nightfall. It did not take the cops long to get there. I filed a report; still not quite believing our car was actually stolen. The first thing the police told me was that this was the number 1 stolen car area in the stolen car capital of the world! Slowly gathering my thoughts, I went back to tell Jack and wait for dear, reliable Val, who had agreed to pick me up after work.

A couple of nurses who overheard my conversation with Jack chimed in that once they each had their cars stolen as well, one of them from the hospital parking lot! "So," I queried, "it would not have made a difference had I been paying outrageous parking fees every day for the past 3 months or so?" It had crossed my mind that maybe, if I had done that, this would not have happened. But no, many car thefts had been reported all around the hospital area. Small consolation! Anyway, Jack took it well; it made him focus on the present and, now that he was starting to talk again, we were able to discuss it at length and actually laugh about it! The Lord was in charge, and we did not worry.

This was not the first car we had stolen in Montreal. My thoughts went back to our first year of marriage when we were living downtown. The hull was found months later totally burnt; everything else had been stripped and, according to police, sold on the black market. But, what about an aging, though thus far reliable, Dodge Spirit? What use would that be to anyone but its owner, I wondered.

When we awoke the next morning the whole scenery was white. If ever I felt like staying home, this was it! However, Liv had an important university project, so we went downtown together in a jaunty white Cavalier supplied by the insurance company. The snow was high and seemed like it had not been plowed; I could hardly differentiate the street from the sidewalk.

15. A Downward Slide

Jack gradually displayed less and less strength and/or motivation in his rehabilitation. One morning as I walked off the elevator, he collapsed right in front of me. He was attempting to take a few steps with the physiotherapist, who that day saw no point in taking him down to the department. Something was wrong! He was brought back to bed. A couple of hours later I was called into the social worker's office. The physiotherapist was there as well, and together they explained that at a conference that morning it was decided that Jack was no longer a candidate for a rehabilitation institute. His progress had deteriorated to a complete standstill.

On the day Jack was transferred from I.C.U. to the ward the social worker had told me that he was considered a long-term care patient. She had explained that, this being an acute care hospital, patients could stay no longer than three months, and that they were actively seeking a nursing home for him. Against my will I had signed an authorization form for them to proceed, but had kept standing in faith, not considering the odds. I believed that Jack would make it back home. His gradual progression and physio sessions had pointed positively towards that, and I had not considered any other option for a moment. The previous month the Quebec Government Health Services Department had already started charging me for his hospital stay.

Tearfully I asked why this conclusion was reached so suddenly and whether Jack's doctor had been part of the decision-making team. Surely the neurological assessment was equally, if not more, important than the physical I mused out loud. They laughed, saying: "You know how hard it is to get a doctor to sit in on one of these meetings?" I retorted instantly that this particular doctor often dropped in on his way to I.C.U. to chat, even though Jack was no longer under his immediate care. I had come to know this doctor well enough to know that not only would he give his expert opinion, but he would expect to be kept abreast of the patient's progress or lack thereof. No matter; they were relentless, informing me that arrangements had already been made for him to go the next morning at 8:30 to a nursing home where French only was spoken. The social worker tersely explained that it was the only one available and, if I wanted to see it, I would have to do so that same afternoon; she would make the appointment for me.

I was speechless. I went upstairs and tried not to look at Jack as my face was red from crying. I did not want to tell him anything yet. Instead, I called the girls to see if they could meet me at the nursing home at 4 o'clock. The place, a former nun's convent, was magnificent. They had allotted Jack a nice bright room to be shared with an English-speaking gentleman. We appreciated that, all the while realizing that once there, his chances of ever coming home would be next to nil.

As we were escorted throughout the building we marvelled at a large ornate meeting hall at the entrance. Liv, in as much shock as I was, choked back tears as she told them that she was in the process of planning her wedding. The thought had struck her that, should her dad not be in a position to get out on her big day, would booking that hall for her wedding be feasible? They instantly agreed. They had never had the privilege of using it for a celebration like that; it would be uplifting for the clientele. Anyway, we had a back-up plan; but we had a much greater vision; we were not giving up!

The girls went on their way and I returned to the General. Approaching the entrance, I walked right into our neurosurgeon! When I asked him if he had heard about the decision to send Jack to a nursing home early in the morning, he was totally surprised and wondered why he had not been notified.

When I described Jack's collapse that morning, he exclaimed: "I should have been informed of that immediately! That has to be checked right away! Sounds to me there is a blockage in the shunt!" He was on his way home; yet it took him but a second to run back in. Within the hour Jack had the MRI test done, and it was confirmed that the shunt was indeed blocked. The fluid that had still been draining from his brain was now blocked, causing a build-up in the brain, thereby affecting both his mental and physical condition!

Phew! I can't describe the relief I felt. Jack was rushed into surgery at 6 the next morning. Then, back into I.C.U.! Imagine the surprise on the social worker's face as I walked on the floor at 8:30! They could not find Jack anywhere and the ambulance was waiting to take him to the nursing home. I calmly told her that I had "accidentally" (I know it was a divine appointment!) bumped into the doctor and that Jack was now in I.C.U. Praise God; He is never late! I did not even want to imagine what could have happened had Jack been sent to the nursing home. His brain would have filled up with blood and, with no physician on the premises, it would not have been diagnosed on time!

That evening, totally spent and close to tears, I was greeted with a wonderful surprise. As I opened the front door, there were all four of my wonderful brood standing around the tape deck singing songs of praise at the top of their lungs! I was so touched and instantly joined in. A nightmare had turned into a wonderful celebration! Our spirits were lifted, again, and we knew that the tide had turned. Thank you, Lord!

I had never quite realized the power of singing out loud to the Lord until this season of testing and standing in faith. At the times when we least feel like singing, that is the time to determine to do so! Oh what joy! Truly, once our heart is set on praising him, regardless of the circumstances, his presence comes in like a flood and fills us with his peace and joy.

"Let everything that has breath praise the Lord. Praise ye the Lord."[24]

---

[24] Ps. 150:6

16. Bugs

As soon as another shunt was inserted to replace the blocked one, an infection set in. I walked in the following day and could not find Jack in I.C.U. The nurse pointed to the isolation room. I was told that they feared he had the "hospital infection:" Staphylococci. This was lethal and very contagious, and they had to keep him in isolation until the test results twenty-four hours later. This, for some reason, did not faze me; I knew that he did not have it.

The next day he was out of isolation. The infection he had was not contagious. A lady in her thirties now occupied the room. She had two small children of about 4 and 6 years of age, who daily visited her with their father. She passed away within 2 weeks from Staphylococci! This is an infection that is contracted in a hospital by patients whose immune systems are low. As sick people have less resistance to fight off diseases they so often (like Jack did when he was initially admitted) get pneumonia and other types of infections while in hospital.

Whenever there was a case of this hospital infection, there was always an aura of secrecy; nurses would barely whisper it so as not to worry other patients and their families. It meant that everyone, including doctors and nurses, had to don a special yellow robe and gloves before entering the room, and discard them immediately afterwards into a special bin outside the room to avoid contamination.

Although Jack was again in Intensive Care, this time he was not hooked up to all the paraphernalia as before. We now regarded this potentially demoralizing situation as a positive experience. After all, it surely had kept him from a much more detrimental fate. Within the week he was back on the ward and from that day forward there was visible progress. He suddenly, spontaneously, started talking about Jesus! Up to that point he had hardly said a word, and then only when necessary. Totally unlike the Jack we knew! Now he was actually preaching! Some of it was garbled, but the love of Jesus shone through him. His spirit was in touch with the Holy Spirit!

17. A Dose of Faith

All through this period the Word of God held us up, and Jack received tapes of the Sunday sermons. Also, Pastor Frey came every week to spend time praying and sharing the Word with Jack. I had found a wonderful place in the main floor hall separating the office annex and the hospital. It was basked in sunshine, and I would push Jack down there every afternoon in one of those old-fashioned cumbersome reclining wheelchairs. It was hard pushing it through the hallways and into the elevator, but it was all worth it just to get Jack out of bed and into a less institutionalized atmosphere. That's where we would pray and chat with the pastor, undisturbed and in peace.

Annie, who was our special prayer partner, also came regularly, as did many others. Jack soon grew quiet again but the Word and praise music kept being fed to him through tapes which played very softly so as not to disturb the other patients.

18. Sowing Seeds

During that time period there were 2 gentlemen in their eighties lying across from each other. Both had suffered a stroke. The one next to Jack seemed to be the more seriously ill of the two; his daughter and son spoke very positive and uplifting words of encouragement to him and gradually we saw him come out of his invisible cocoon. Once he did, his family hired a caregiver to sit with him during the night as he tended to get confused. This caring person happened to be another lovely lady in our church, who had also been visiting and praying for Jack. Now she was silently praying for both until this gentleman was transferred to rehab a couple of weeks later!

Meanwhile, one of the other gentleman's daughters, a nurse at this hospital, also happened to be one of our neighbours.[iii] Her mom came in every day with homemade soup. He would take the odd sip but after a couple of days refused to eat anything at all. This went on for 2 to 3 weeks and the family soon tearfully realized that this was the end. Maybe his condition was worse than it seemed and he knew it. On the day he only had hours to live, I asked if I could read some verses from the Torah (The Hebrew name for the Old Testament) as the family was Jewish, and they agreed. I was urged by the Holy Spirit to read:

"Fear thou not; for I am with thee; be not dismayed; for I am thy God. I will strengthen thee; yea, I will help thee; yea I will uphold thee with the right hand of my

55

*righteousness. For I the Lord thy God will hold thy right
hand, saying unto thee, Fear not; I will help thee.*"[25]

Across from Jack was a man in his early fifties. He was a
Scott with a good sense of humour, and he loved to talk. He did not
seem "sick" and actually did not belong on the Neurosurgery floor.
He had developed an infection on a skin graft performed as an
outpatient day surgery procedure that morning, and the doctor
wanted him to stay overnight to monitor the situation. He
explained that for previous grafts he had always been prescribed an
antibiotic to be taken a day prior to the operation, but not this time.

Anyway, he was in good spirits; and Jack perked up when he
discovered that they had a mutual friend. As soon as this chap
realized that, he picked up the phone and told his friend to get over
there and visit Jack. Sure enough, that same evening he walked in.
No doubt he was shocked at Jack's condition, but he was very
gracious and witty, and it did Jack a world of good. It was
someone from the recent past in the business world outside, and it
helped jog Jack's memory.

Our Scottish friend got to know the family and hear the
prayers and words of faith, but he was not receptive to the gospel.
He did agree for me to pray for him, as I did for everyone the Lord
brought us in contact with. One morning suddenly the curtains
were drawn around his bed and an emergency team ran in. I found
out later that he had an embolism in his lung. He was rushed up to
another floor. That was the last time we saw him.

One Sunday afternoon, while praying for Jack with some
friends, I heard a commotion and noticed a woman entering the
room, and then quietly retreating. A few minutes later when I
enquired at the desk, Sylvia, whose "mom" we had met and who
was now Jack's regular caregiver,[iv] informed me that Jack's
Scottish friend had just passed away and that his wife wanted me
to go up and see her. I sat with her for quite a while, silently
praying and comforting her until her family arrived. It had been so

---

[25] Isa. 41:11,13

sudden and unexpected. I went to the funeral home and kept in touch for a while but eventually lost contact due to her work schedule and my long days at the hospital.[v]

The Lord is wonderful. Seeds were sown. That's all he asks us to do sometimes, depending on the situation and the timing in a person's life. The Holy Spirit does the rest. Mary, a lady who had suffered a minor stroke, was receptive to hear about the love of God, and promptly accepted Jesus as her Lord and Saviour. We prayed together for her recovery, and she could hardly believe that she was released within a few days!

19. Once Lost, Now Found

Three weeks after our car's disappearance we got a call from the Police Department of Joliette, a small community about twenty kilometers east of Montreal. The car had been used in a bank robbery the previous night and left abandoned in a back alley. They insisted that it be picked up within twenty-four hours. I was so relieved as time was running out for the rental car, and spending time and money shopping for a replacement was definitely not on our agenda. Alas, the insurance company informed me that towing the car was not in the contract! What to do!?

The next day we woke up to sleet. It was so bad that I cancelled my daily visit with Jack, much to his chagrin. Everyone stayed home; the roads were crusted with ice. By mid afternoon it eased off a little, turning partially to rain. Deane and I decided to make a dash for it as we were both home and on any given day it would be difficult to find a second driver due to exams and/or jobs. We detoured via the island of Laval, which was less traveled than the direct but treacherous autoroute across the island of Montreal. That turned out to be a wise decision as there was no one on the road and, though slushy, the pavement was free of ice. Deane and I enjoyed our time together. It took us about an hour to get there, the country road off the highway being quite icy.

The policeman on duty was surprised to see us and apologized for the condition of the car, which was covered with a yellowish dust. He explained that it had been dusted for fingerprints and he offered the hose and soap if we wanted to wash it, which Deane promptly did. The inside was also a mess and the contents of the trunk were gone. Deane drove it home and I followed in the Cavalier. By now dusk had fallen, and I was grateful to be following her lights on the country road, as my night vision was not the greatest and the white of the road was barely distinguishable from the snowy shoulder. By the time we reached the island of Montreal the precipitation had stopped and the traffic moved smoothly. Praise the Lord!

We were proud of ourselves and happy to have the car back. It wasn't until two days later that the realization sunk in that the insurance very definitely should have paid for the return of the car. The agent had neglected to tell me that, if I had paid a towing company, they would have reimbursed part or all of it. I never did get a full answer on that and, due to the urgency to pick it up along with everything else that was going on, my mind was in a standstill mode. Subsequent to a friend's unexpected call, telling me how she had been blessed with great service, I promptly transferred to her insurance company. This new company is known to go out of their way to help their clientele and at considerably better rates for both household and car insurance! Ha! Ha! I would not have considered switching if it were not for the experience of getting less than satisfactory treatment and having another company recommended at the same time!

> *"And we know that all things work together for good to them that love God, to them who are the called according to his purpose."*[26]

---

[26] Rom. 10:28

20. Double Blessings

At the end of January Liv and Val went on a week's Caribbean cruise with the Toronto Blue Jays! They had been invited to accompany a Christian baseball player's family as babysitters. We had all come to know this family well over the past several summers through Jack's baseball connections. The two previous years, while the catcher was playing on the Montreal Expos team, Liv and Val had become close with their two children. This was exciting, and I was so happy for both of them to get the chance to recoup before the busy upcoming months while on their winter break.

Jack had always been involved in his favourite pastime: baseball. He had coached bantam, midget and junior levels, scouted for the New York Mets, was interim chaplain for the Montreal Expos and their visiting teams, and had attended a lot of games with the girls over the years.

During Liv's absence, Deane and Mark suddenly announced: "Mom, we will be ready soon." "When," I exclaimed, "what do you mean 'soon'?" "Very soon," they answered, "definitely by the fall, if not sooner." I gasped. It was not news to me that they wanted to get married, but somehow I could deal with only one wedding at a time; certainly not two the same year! Another joint family meeting was in order.

Deane and I met with Mark and his family around their kitchen table. We attentively listened to their excited plans of how they had saved up money; and they both had good jobs, with Mark preparing to set up a security company. They did not want anything lavish; they would be happy with a very small service, no fancy wedding gown and no hoop-la! When the feasibility of a joint wedding came up, they both exclaimed: "Oh no!" They knew

how particular Liv was about her wedding to the finest detail!
Different scenarios were brainstormed and we left with a long list
of ideas to digest, discuss and pray about.

As soon as Liv heard about it, she became very excited and
actually offered to have a joint wedding! However, she stipulated,
it would still be her dream wedding with her colour scheme of
burgundy and off-white, and so forth. Deane with her gentle and
easy-going nature had no trouble going along with that.

They instantly decided to add Mark's siblings, Nancy and
Izaak, as bridesmaid and best man respectively. Liv's bridesmaid
was Karen, and Sergio's best man his brother, Gustavo. Val was
chosen to be maid-of-honour for both brides. Phew, that was easy!
Thank you, Lord! Seeing Deane's whole face light up as she
modeled her chosen gown the following Saturday confirmed it all
to me. She expressed that she felt like a princess; and indeed she
was!

21. Rehabilitation

Early in March Jack was transferred to a rehabilitation facility. This, too, was sprung on us without any warning. What a happy day! This meant that Jack now was a candidate for more extensive physio- and occupational therapies. I loved the fact that I did not have to travel so far, could park freely on the premises, and enjoy the nice bright atmosphere better than the somber hospital setting.

Jack at first was apprehensive about his new surroundings and possibly of failing to meet real or perceived expectations. His mind was still very preoccupied, but the good news was that now he was eating better. The personnel were concerned about his little appetite but I assured them that he indeed was doing very well.

Here, too, the Lord had a Christian nurse available. She had heard our pastor pray for Jack and enquired if it was O.K. for her to pray for him, too. As well, a friend of my author-friend worked there as a caregiver.

As the weather improved I wheeled Jack every afternoon out to the lovely park on the premises, where he would practice wheelchair maneuvering around the paths. Learning for the first time to ride a wheelchair was not only traumatic for him but, with the limited use of his left arm and leg and the lack of overall strength, it was a major challenge. The rehabilitation progressed slowly but steadily.

22. Preparing for the Big Day

All the wedding preparations just fell into place with minimal effort. The Lord's hand was on it all the way. Everything from the florist, photographer, music and invitation cards came recommended by friends, saving us a lot of time-consuming searching and comparing. We were exceptionally blessed and pleased with everything.

The florist was a jovial Dutchman with a large greenhouse smack in the middle of the city. Over the many years the city had sprung up all around his beautiful garden patch. As it was just down the street, the girls and I took Jack out to help make the choices for the bridal bouquets, church décor and table decorations. It was such a joy feasting on the lovely hues and aromas in this huge indoor garden. Their service was wonderful. They truly went out of their way to make suggestions and even designing the table decorations.

Jack started getting in the mood a bit more, and on his own initiative started practicing his father-of-the-brides' toast. Even the physiotherapist and nurses got into the act, especially when they heard it was going to be a double wedding. They explained that I would need a private orderly to help with Jack, and they already had one in mind! He had served his internship there recently and they all had been exceptionally impressed with him. They gave me his telephone number; we clicked right away, and yes, he would book that date for us! Wow, even that fell into place before it had even entered my mind!

All the people we dealt with were excited about the prospect of catering to a double wedding. The mood now became truly festive. There were wedding showers to attend, final preparations to be discussed with the maitre D', guest lists to be checked and invitations to be addressed. The latter was no mean feat! We had agreed to restrict the number of guests to a hundred for Liv's wedding. Now, for 3 families and their friends that number was upped by only twenty-five more. It was not an easy task; everyone had to be very selective. There was quite a bit of rubbing out and adding being done until the brides and grooms were finally satisfied that their family members and friends were represented. Furthermore, we invited friends, acquaintances and church members to attend the wedding ceremony and a mini reception at the church.

Everyone had a job to do. Sergio's mom, Solange, offered to coordinate the outfits for little Dillon, the ring bearer, and his 2 cousins, Martin and Karlos. Val's mom, Suzanne, took on the fitting and sewing of the gowns for the bridal party. Deane was in charge of the wedding cake, Mark managed the guest list and designed the place settings, Sergio was dispatched to tuxedo and limousine rentals, and Liv looked after all the finer details of church decorations, and so on. My 2 gals and Val also found time to accompany me on my dress-hunting escapade. Good thing, too, as it was Deane who found my dream gown while I had my eye on something else. I would have missed it completely, and that would have been a shame. This one was totally "made for me!"

Most of the wedding preparations had to be done in the evenings due to our busy schedules, but it all got done just in the nick of time. Liv and I even made time to lay down new vinyl tiles in the kitchen. Everything had to be spick and span. Where the time and especially my energy came from I can only attribute to the Lord; in the natural it was not there! Alas, Sergio, who had originally offered to do the job, had a change in shift and was working nights at just the wrong time. But we soon got the hang of it and, working as a team over a period of three late evenings, we enjoyed warm mother-daughter fellowship. After all, there had been precious little time for that with projects, studies and upcoming exams, on top of all the other tensions and deadlines.

23. Showers of Blessing

That spring was wonderful. Jack and I were out in the little park just about every day. On Sundays after church we would all pick up a fast food order, and partake together in the park with Dad, who enjoyed the treats. It was a great time getting up-to-date on all the news and his latest accomplishments.

In the midst of the storm the Lord had come up with a fantastic surprise. On my birthday I was blessed out of the blue with a wonderful inheritance! My eighty-eight-year-old auntie Ann decided to dole out her inheritance to her family before her time to be with the Lord! We just couldn't believe it; we were ecstatic. If ever we needed an extra financial boost, it was then! Praise the Lord for dear Auntie Ann.

One of those Sundays in the beginning of May, a business associate of Mark's came to church with him. He had driven from Toronto in his Pontiac Bonneville, which was a few years old. It was time to trade it in, and he had offered it to Mark for a price lower than that listed, wanting him to have it for his business. However, having just overhauled and re-painted his own car, Mark retorted immediately: "Ann will need a big car to transport Jack. Offer it to her for the same amazing price you quoted me."

I stood aback when Mark told me about it and gave him a big hug for his thoughtfulness. The Dodge Spirit was old and since its return it did not seem to have the same 'oomph' it had before. I test-drove the Bonneville to the rehab centre to show Jack and to get his opinion and approval. It was love at first sight. The trunk was big enough to transport a wheelchair and more, the wide doors provided ample room for transferring Jack in and out and, we had it in time for the wedding! This was such a wise observation on Mark's part. Having been living one day at a time, I had not yet considered all the things needed to be in place for Jack's return home.

I had come to know Steve, who had visited Jack in the hospital a few times. He was more than happy to give us the same amazing deal he had offered Mark. Jack agreed, and the deal went through immediately. It was a true blessing (still is!) especially as, once more, I did not have to lift a finger to decide what kind to get, or where to start looking. At that time I had no energy for anything but the concerns of the day at hand. I would leave everything in God's hands.

> *"But seek ye first the kingdom of God, and his righteousness; and all these things shall be added unto you. Take therefore no thought for the morrow; for the morrow shall take thought for the things of itself. Sufficient unto the day is the evil thereof."*[27]

The Dodge was passed on to another friend of Mark's, who was studying mechanics at the time. He enjoyed it but for a few weeks until suddenly the motor gave up; its "spirit" literally left. We just could not believe it! It could have left me stranded with Jack in the car! Thank you, Lord!

> *"He hath made every thing beautiful in his time: also he hath set the world in their heart, so that no man can find out the work that God maketh from the beginning to the end."*[28]

Truly, God shows up when you least expect it. He is the God of surprises. When everything looks darkest, he sheds his light. What's more, he is never late!

The day of the wedding rehearsal finally arrived! I took Jack to the church, where we finally met the orderly. What a delightful, obliging and capable young man! We could well imagine why the

---

[27] Matt. 6:33-34
[28] Eccl. 3:11

nurses had singled him out. Everything went well, and we arranged to meet up with him and the bridal party at the top landing of the back stairs on the big day. He would return Jack in our car to the rehab centre after the picture taking and reception at the church. After a short rest, he would bring him to the reception at the golf course.

On the eve of the wedding Wilf and Sue came to visit Jack. It was a bittersweet reunion as Jack was a bit uptight about not yet being his happy-go-lucky self for the wedding, but we had a good time. That evening at home was super hectic. There was so much to do until well after midnight. Nobody realized how many last minute details could suddenly pop up.

24. Double Celebration

The big day finally came and everything was perfect and on time. After the hairdos, make-ups and home and garden photographs, I left to pick up Dad while the girls prepared for the limousine ride to church. Jack looked wonderful in his tuxedo and he was ready to go. I felt like the belle of the ball myself as all the staff and a lot of the patients gave compliments. It brought a moment of excitement in their lives as well.

Here we are: Jack and I are on the little landing at the side door of the church. We hear some rustling at the base of the stairs and I bend over the banister to have a look. There comes Liv, with her head down as she is holding up her gown, carefully watching every step as it curves around onto the landing. Straightening up as she reaches the top step, she looks straight into the eyes of her dad. She hesitates for a moment; then rushes into his outstretched arms, her eyes welling up at the impact of knowing he is there for her, looking like a million dollars in his tux. A divine moment!

While I am hugging Liv, who is desperately trying to contain herself, up comes Val around the curve. She, too, is startled and misty-eyed at the sight of Jack. A moment's pause; then she bravely takes charge in her maid-of-honour role and, taking a tissue from me, proceeds to carefully dab Liv's eyes, trying to preserve as much of the make-up as possible. Deane is now gliding up the staircase, daintily lifting her crinolined gown. As Liv and Val make way for her to step onto the tiny landing she, straightening up, coming face to face with her father, promptly bursts into tears.

In the meantime the pastor's wife, in charge of directing the wedding party, has come up the main staircase across the hall with the rest of the wedding party. Peeking in, poised to give the command for the wedding march, she encounters three pairs of teary eyes not quite ready for the grand entrance. It's an awesome moment for all of us. The march can wait, for a minute at least, until all the eyes are dabbed and some composure is restored. Through the crack of the door I notice that the church, which holds over four hundred people, is packed, and the video camera is ready to roll.

The moment is here. The tiny ringbearer and his entourage are being set in step to the wedding march. As Jack comes into view, with me pushing the wheelchair down the aisle, the whole congregation spontaneously explodes into a standing ovation. This was not rehearsed! Only a moment ago I thought we were more or less composed. Taken aback, I hesitate momentarily. Surprise and awe are almost instantly intermingled with an "oh no!" as out of the corner of my eye I notice the two cousins desperately trying to persuade Dillon to get back in line. The little guy, also temporarily "undone" by this outpouring of love, refuses to go on. No time to be concerned about protocol or a few tears flowing! These are our friends; they all know about the trials Jack has been through and most of them have been steadfastly praying for his recovery.

The ovation is unto the Lord for having made it possible for Jack to proudly give his two daughters away. It is an intense moment of awe, love, jubilation and amazement all at the same time; it will remain in our hearts forever.

The young trio are gently guided back in line by Mrs. Frey. The aisle is so long! Out of the corner of my eye I see so many old, familiar faces; yet at the same time I am desperately trying to keep my composure, look straight ahead, and keep in step with the music. At last we're at the front. I turn the wheelchair sideways and look back at the other parents and the bridal party. Here comes Liv, beaming, but her eyes are glistening behind the veil. Deane follows with tears flowing unashamedly down her cheeks, yet her head held high and her eyes steadfastly on her groom at the altar.

*"And who gives this bride away" the pastor asks. "I do,"
comes the clear, firm reply as Jack proudly looks up at Liv beside
him. He then turns to Deane on his left and dittoes his reply to the
pastor's second query. The two brides then lift their veils and each
give him a big kiss.*

The beauty of the double ceremony was very touching, and we
were proud of the way Pastor Frey had designed it. It was truly
anointed and flowed fluently from one couple to the other. The
soloist was outstanding. Janet and her pastor husband John had
ministered in the church where Liv, Deane and Val had spent
their formative years. They were now pastoring a church in
Ontario but their sons and our gals had kept in touch over the
years. She was Liv's perfect choice for soloist. When Liv called to
announce her wedding, Janet had uttered a spontaneous "yes" to
her hesitant question as to whether she might be available. It so
happened that they would be in Montreal for a conference that very
weekend and the timing of the ceremony fit perfectly into their
schedule! They always had a close relationship, and Janet had
specifically prayed for her to be blessed with a godly husband.

The return from the altar was different! We all literally danced
down that aisle, totally jubilant, to the beat of a celebratory praise
song. It set the tone for a wonderful celebration of what the Lord
had done.

It was a wonderful reunion, seeing so many friends and
acquaintances, some of which we had not seen for years! The
reception line that followed in the downstairs hall seemed endless
as literally hundreds filed by and loved on Jack. It was awesome to
hear that almost to a man they expressed how they had been
touched by our faith and had grown in their own faith just by
praying for and following Jack's progress! We had no idea how
Jack's ordeal had impacted so many! It gave us great affirmation
and encouragement. What a testimony of the Lord's goodness!

Jack had a nap for a couple of hours, giving him a bit of
respite after the exciting but exhausting event. He subsequently
arrived at the golf club reception in time for the family

photographs. Meanwhile, I enjoyed the beautiful facility, sharing with family and friends watching the different photo shoots.

The photographer clearly enjoyed setting up the different scenarios, both separate couples and all four together. It was a leisurely gorgeous, warm day. The weather forecaster obviously did not know that we had prayed for a perfect day! He had forecast rain! In fact that morning it was threatening but by noon it had cleared. The thin haze was perfect for pictures, according to our photographer. It was neither too cool nor too hot. It was too early in the season for bugs.

In the excitement and in anticipation of his upcoming speech, Jack did not have much of an appetite. I reminded him of a story we had heard once of how Queen Elizabeth would move the food across her plate, pretending to eat, or just eat a few morsels, giving the impression that she was enjoying the meal. It worked, and we were both able to laugh about it. Finally, his moment! He was just great and got a wonderful applause. That seemed to loosen him up and he was ready for the father and the brides' first dance! He swung his wheelchair back and forth to the beat as his two pride-and-joys proudly danced together with him!

Jack was ready to leave after doing the rounds, chatting with the guests, and good-bye hugs with the brides. As had been arranged, Mark's brother went along to take him back and return the car for me. Everything had gone just perfectly. The music and oodles of desserts kept rolling until after midnight and at last it was time to see our brides and their grooms off to their honeymoons. We were both so proud of our two daughters and two sons. We did not consider them as sons-in-law, but truly our sons.

25. The Empty Nest

The focus had been so much on the excitement of the upcoming wedding and Jack's recuperation that I had not given conscious thought to the fact that my girls would not be coming home! This was not just a vacation; they were really gone! As we were watching them drive off, Sue proffered: "Ann, it's going to be different as you experience the empty nest. Feel free to call us anytime when you get overwhelmed!" I politely thanked her, imagining their feeling of loss when Allison, their only child, got married exactly a year earlier, but could not relate to what she was saying.

It was strange going to bed in an empty house, though. I would suddenly wake up during the night, hearing a soft, wailing sound. Flicking on the lights as I slowly, very cautiously inched along, it would always stop before I could get very far. I could not make out for some time where it came from until one morning, coming into the kitchen for breakfast I realized it was the fridge thermostat starting up! It would not last long. Surely it had never done that before! It was a brand new fridge that Liv and I had picked out to replace the old one when we were laying the tiles. The clocks, too, were ticking so loudly. What was wrong with them; I had never heard them before!

And how I suddenly missed Chinook, our lovely, gorgeous Alaskan Malamute. He had passed away the previous year from old age. We had all missed him so much but then with Jack's hospitalization, even though I missed him, I had felt relief that I did not have to walk him twice a day, as he was used to. He needed a lot of exercise and Jack and him were a team around the neighbourhood every morning and again exactly at 7 p.m. After the evening news, Chinook would be at the door barking, ready to go!

He would not have understood where his master had gone or the change in schedule. How much did I suddenly miss his head on my lap with his long bushy tail wagging against my leg!

The third evening I came home emotionally drained. Not only had the wedding and all the events leading up to it taken a toll on me, but I had just found out that Jack was not progressing as well as expected. He seemed to have hit a plateau, which was not sufficient for his transfer back home. The prognosis was: "Back to the hospital!" "That's not an option!" I had gasped. I explained to the team that hospitalization would most certainly do him in completely, both physically and emotionally. They were very understanding and assured me that they would look into all options within the next week together with our local C.L.S.C. (home care group), and get back to me.

The stillness and emptiness hit me like a ton of bricks as I walked in the door that evening! It just all caved in on me. My girls were gone; my husband was gone, my dog was gone! I felt like a widow: totally alone in the world! It suddenly hit me why they had termed it the empty nest syndrome! Really, really empty with seemingly nothing to replace the loss! I picked up the phone and called Sue; yeah, the empty nest wasn't just a cute description of having your home all to yourself; it's like a deep hole full of nothing! I shed some tears; then cried some more. After a while I opened my Bible and had a chat with the Lord. He just quietly said:

"I shall never leave you nor forsake you"[29]

and

"In the world ye shall have tribulation: but be of good cheer; I have overcome the world."[30]

---

[29] Heb. 13:5
[30] John 16:33

Glory to God! I had turned my eyes temporarily on the circumstances instead of immediately on God. Thank you, Lord; you're always there to affirm, strengthen, and carry me as with wings of eagles!

That week a well-known evangelist was in town. Our church was involved in his ministry and Jack agreed to come with me to the Thursday evening crusade. It was wonderful and very late by the time we got back, but we agreed to return on the Saturday morning for a ministry breakfast. We arrived there real early and got to sit front row centre with some of our church family. When they started praying for people, we were up like a flash. Jack, in fact, got prayed for several times as he would wheel himself back into the prayer line for more! The Lord's presence was very tangible, and we trusted the Lord with all our hearts to do exceedingly abundantly above all that we could ask or think.

> *"Now unto him that is able to do exceedingly abundantly above all that we ask or think, according to the power that worketh in us, unto him be glory in the church by Christ Jesus throughout all ages, world without end. Amen"*[31]

We both trusted that the Lord had begun something new in Jack, even though there was no immediate physical manifestation of healing.

---

[31] Eph. 3:20-21

26. Homecoming

A joint meeting of the hospital staff and the C.L.S.C. was scheduled for the following week. The newlyweds were back from their respective honeymoons and we all did some brainstorming together. Sergio, who was at the meeting, declared that he and Mark would be working as a unit to do whatever it took to make Jack functional at home. We were advised that the C.L.S.C. would be visiting our home to ascertain wheelchair accessibility, etc. and Sergio's friend, Kent, helped him build a ramp up the two steps from the driveway to the walkway and another one at the front door. He was a real godsend and did an excellent job in his spare time to have it finished just in time for the visit. He had never even met Jack!

The combined hospital and follow-up teams were absolutely superb. They truly went out of their way, recommending that Jack get the maximum daily orderly assistance of 2 hours per day every day for bathing, getting dressed and some exercises. They also stipulated in the report that the orderly would have to engage Jack in conversation and/or game playing to help him come out of his introspective state of mind. We were so happy about that.

Jack had expressed that, although he knew most of the people at the wedding by name, he had no recollection of the circumstances as to how he knew them! This was evidence that the short-term memory loss was still there big-time, that it bothered him terribly, and was the major cause of his brooding. We had always been able to count on Jack's keen memory and awareness of all the latest news. Conversation and interactive play with an outsider as part of a daily routine would help to gradually re-hone his memory and interest in current events. We were so happy and Jack, who also took part in the meeting, could hardly believe that he was actually going home within a few days! We thanked everyone involved.

The head nurse, physio- and occupational therapists, along with the head occupational therapist at our C.L.S.C., worked as a team and were amazingly sensitive to my Jack's needs. Sensing my limited strength and the lack of instant access to our "sons," the recommendation was to have a back-up person nearby to help with transfers.

Again, the Lord came through! While discussing Jack's situation with our next door neighbours, their seventeen-year-old son offered to help out whenever necessary, day or night! A serious, affable young man, Andrew was genuinely concerned about Jack's progress and he would be home most of the time during that summer. He was eager and genuine about his commitment, wanting to learn exactly what was required of him and how to do it correctly. He volunteered to come with me to a physiotherapy session, where he practiced with the therapist.

Everything was ready for Jack's homecoming and I was so grateful for everyone's help, concern and the assurance of instant assistance from next door. For the first couple of weeks I needed to call on my young assistant about once a day; he was always there on the spot. Eventually I got the hang of doing the transfers alone as Jack also became stronger and more adept at doing his part. The hardest part was going up and down the ramps with the wheelchair. They were only temporary and a little too steep due to limitations of the width of the driveway and turning room for the wheelchair at the door.

Mark, in the meantime, had put aside time to help me clear out excess "junk" that had accumulated over the years in the laundry room in order to make room for a gym! He had weight lifting and body building equipment at his parents' home, and his vision was to have it set up here for Jack to work out. I realized with a shock that I had become a packrat, keeping things just in case they might come in handy some day. Mark assured me in his wisdom that what I don't need today, someone else can be blessed with, and the Lord would be my provider whenever I would be in need of anything! How right he was! I felt ashamed about hoarding so much and started making piles, including one for the Sally Ann. Finally, after a couple of days of doing this, Mark could not hold it in any longer and blurted out: "Who is Sally Ann?" It was so funny; I explained to him that it was a nickname for the Salvation Army.

The goal was to strengthen Jack's weak side and to practice with his walker. He was not able yet to transfer alone from his wheelchair to the walker or to walk alone with it, and I wasn't strong enough to help him do it. Either Mark or Sergio, whoever was available any given day, would come and help Jack down the stairs and work out with him. Both of them had body building experience and knew what exercises would strengthen specific muscles. As a backup, when both were working, Kaz volunteered so that Jack would never miss a single day! Jack liked and appreciated it, even though it took a lot out of him physically. I was so immensely proud of, and thankful for, the extended family the Lord provided for us.

27. Home Care

The situation with the first orderly we had was quite a challenge. He was not the talkative type nor affable in any way. He did the absolute minimum and would not converse with Jack on any topic. As it had been explained to us that orderlies were not professionals and, therefore, to have patience with them, we did not complain. One morning, hearing a scream from the bathroom, I ran in to find him spraying Jack in the face despite his repeated pleas not to do so! The orderly insisted that was the way he was trained to wash a patient's face! Although he agreed not to do it again, I called the agency, only to find out that he was "the best we've got!" We were subsequently referred to another agency. The next fellow we got was kind, but inefficient. He literally needed to be trained, even with his own personal hygiene. Yet he was compliant and gentle, and Jack felt a little more secure with him.

That whole summer Jack was still very quiet but started to be more attentive to the news, Christian music and teaching tapes. He came to church, where the ushers gingerly carried him up the long stairway, and had visits with the newlyweds, who proudly showed him their apartments. Almost every day I would take him for a drive around the island of Montreal in order to reintroduce him to the world he used to be so much a part of. He still could not connect most of the past to the present.

Every effort would take a lot of physical and emotional strength out of my Jack. After his bath he would need to lie down for an hour. Long afternoon naps and early bedtime were the order of the day. Furthermore, he did not want any visitors whatsoever. It wasn't easy for me; I literally became a recluse as I needed to be nearby at all times, and tried to do my shopping while the orderly was there. The ramps were hard on the back but, since it had to be done, I mastered getting my man up and down them as best I could. The kids were all great; they came over a lot. It was reassuring that they did not live far from home.

28. Back Again

Some physical progress had been made, but Jack's mind was still absorbed. The hospital where Jack had his angiogram called again; this time at home. They had called repeatedly regarding the urgency of a second angiogram procedure to tighten the loop on the aneurysm in order to stop the leakage. However, I had kept refusing as Jack's condition while still in hospital had been too fragile. Also, his neurosurgeon, whom I had consulted each time they called, had offered neither a nay or a yeah. It was a routine procedure, done on an outpatient basis, I was told. Jack and I discussed it and we called the surgeon for his decision. At that time the Neurosurgery Department of the Montreal General was closed due to more cutbacks, and Jack's doctor had transferred to this very hospital, working in close liaison with the pioneer neuroradiologist who had looped the aneurysm. This time he confirmed the importance of having this procedure done as Jack was now home, physically stronger, and in need of it.

The day before the angiogram my brother John and his wife Bev spent the afternoon with us. They had come down from their home in Northern Ontario and it was a great reunion together with the whole family. We did not tell anyone about our decision except Liv and Sergio on their way out that day, being the last ones to leave. No need to cause possible concern, we figured. We prayed together for a good outcome. After all, it was only an outpatient thing and Jack felt positive about it.

We had trusted the Lord for everything. I had felt an immediate "Yes" when I received the phone call; yet now I was starting to get an ever-so-slight check in my spirit about this. At bedtime I told Jack that, if I did not wake up on time without setting the alarm for the early morning appointment, I would cancel. He silently nodded. Jack nudged me awake from a deep sleep; it was time to go! "Oh, Jack!" I thought; "you would have to wake up early!" But, that's what we had agreed to do. I asked him again if he felt sure about this and the answer was: "Yes, let's go!"

On the way off the expressway we passed another hospital and Jack pointed out that was where a local personality had lost his leg due to the flesh-eating disease. I said: "Jack, I can go straight back home, if you want." "No," came the reply. The time went very slowly waiting for our turn to get a hospital card, then being checked by a nurse. Before being disrobed and put on a stretcher, Jack signed the release form himself. As we arrived at the Radiology Department, a resident doctor met us and explained in detail everything that could go wrong, including an embolism. This time I wanted to hightail it out of there, insisting: "Jack, this is not worth it!" His retort: "When I come back, I'll be healed!" as they whisked him away.

I was told it would take about an hour. I went into the parking lot and sat in the car enjoying the warm sun while quietly praying. I knew Jack wanted his memory back; that was at the very root of his misery. It did not even matter to him whether he would ever walk again! He felt that this procedure could be the answer to his prayer and I was powerless to deny him that. It was a chance we needed to take and all the while I knew the Lord would bring him through it.

When I returned, the neuroradiologist was waiting for me in the hall. Jack had suffered an embolism! He told me that he had a drug that would dissolve it but that he needed my authorization. For another hour I paced up and down the hall praying, while a procession of stretchers filled the hallway. I realized that it was my husband in there holding up these precious people. I felt like shouting and telling everyone what had happened and to get out of there while they still could. But the Lord covered me in his Peace, as with a warm cloak around my shoulders. The doctor afterwards explained that homocysteine, a whitish, sticky substance in the artery, had caused the blockage when they passed the angiogram through it. They never even got anywhere near the aneurysm site!

Once stable, Jack was wheeled to a room across the hall, where he had to lay still while they clamped his angiogram site. I noticed when they finally allowed me in, that the other patients all had gauze between the sponge-tipped clamp and the skin. Jack's sponge was directly on his skin and I wondered out loud if this was hygienic. The nurse assured me that this was "procedure" but I did not get an answer as to why the other patients in the room had the gauze. When checked about half an hour later there was still no scab forming. I then learned that Jack had been given heparin, a blood-thinning drug to prevent further clotting. Knowing that he had had a daily shot of that at the General as well, I was familiar with it.

As the scabbing proceeded very slowly due to the blood thinner, it was decided to keep Jack overnight in Intermediate Neurological Intensive Care for monitoring. I felt so bad for Jack! I hugged him and promised never ever to take him to a hospital again! He agreed. He was finally released around 5 the next afternoon.

Jack was so happy to be back home but he was exhausted. The following day he practically slept all day. The resident called to check if I had administered the blood thinning medication he had prescribed. He was kind and concerned and gave me his cell phone number, in case we needed him. I told him right away that the site was still oozing, describing the condition in detail. His answer was that this was "all right and normal".

Friday September 3rd Jack had a high temperature during the night, continuing that morning despite the cold compresses and Tylenol I had given him. He did not get out of bed and refused to have any orderly (I had called off the last orderly and asked the agency not to send anyone else until Jack was feeling better). The physio, who arrived for her weekly workout with Jack called the C.L.S.C. for a nurse to come over but it was the start of Labour Day Weekend. Nobody showed up. I called the resident doctor. The neuroradiologist happened to be in conference with him and together they assured me: "We're not at all concerned; he must have contracted a virus."

During the long Labour Day weekend Jack continued to have fevers during the night but they eased off during the day and he was up for longer periods of time. Ever since his homecoming Jack had been listless. It was hard for me to determine whether this was due to the aftermath of the embolism, the medication, or the "virus." Jack was otherwise not complaining and kept saying that it did not hurt and it was all right. Knowing my guy, I was also aware that he did not want to go back to the hospital.

The day after the long weekend I expressed my continued concern to the doctor about the night fevers. Again he told me not to worry; that there had never been an infection in an angiogram site but that, if I had any concerns, I should bring Jack to the hospital. I told him that I had an appointment with our family doctor the following day, and that I would ask him to check Jack as well.

Mark helped me the next morning to get Jack in the car; he was too weak and I was not able to do it alone. Although he again had a fever during the night, he did not have one that morning. The doctor declared there was no infection, but he would not look at the wound. I asked him how he could be sure. He just raised his eyebrows. Both Jack and I felt a sense of relief, hoping that he was finally getting over this malaise. That evening the foursome were all there and Jack was up. When Sergio put him to bed for me, Jack felt a "snap" at the site.

29. Please Lord, Not Again!

Waking up around 5:30 on the 9th I heard Jack babbling in delirium with a high fever. I noticed his wound was oozing again, which it had not done for a couple of days. This time, after the doctors' reassurances, I thought the delirium might have something to do with the brain shunt. Was it clogged up again? I gave Jack Tylenol and cold compresses, got myself together, and at 9:00 called 911.

When the ambulance arrived I told them Jack's history and asked them to take him to the hospital where both his neuroradiologist and neurosurgeon were. I was convinced he had a neurological condition at the time. They told me flat out that they "don't go that far." I knew that an ambulance had to take the patient to the nearest hospital in an emergency, but this was not a life-and-death situation and by then the fever had subsided.

Once at our local hospital, the Emergency doctor consulted with the neurosurgeon over the phone, and agreed to do the preliminary testing first before deciding to transfer. That took hours. At noon the visibly disturbed doctor informed me that the blood sample was lost! The department was bulging to the brim with patients on stretchers and they had found a more isolated spot for Jack at the end of a hallway. Finally, around 5 o'clock, with a wave from the doctor, we were sent off. He wished us a good hospital, unlike their own, which was in chaos.

We were in the middle of rush hour, moving bumper to bumper from the West Island right through downtown to the east-end. During the afternoon I had noticed that Jack's wound was now purplish and ugly looking. It had not been like that before. On the way I found out that the protocol for ambulance drivers was to go to the hospital of the client's choice, except in an emergency.

More cultures and tests were conducted upon arrival and Jack was administered Vancomycin immediately. I recognized this drug. It was the medication Jack was given at the General when it was thought that he had the Staphylococci infection. I felt relieved as I knew that this was a strong drug that would "cure" anything that could be wrong.

A whole day was lost and this time I was very, very concerned about a host of things. The blood test results would take 24 hours. Oh no! That would bring us into another weekend! I suddenly realized I had to update the kids as to what was happening. Kaz happened to be in town and arranged to pick me up. Praise God! At that point I didn't even know what to do. I was prepared to just stay there until they talked sense into me.

I was completely numb. Lord, I prayed, please don't let this be a serious situation! I could not possibly ever go through that again! I heard the Lord saying that it was a whole lot easier to give up and let go than to stand in faith!

On Friday afternoon the results were conclusive: it was not a virus; it was the Staphylococci infection! This was the dreaded hospital infection, and here the doctors had been playing around with it for over a week refusing to believe it could even be an infection! The shunt was fine and all other tests came back negative. I was introduced to the vascular surgeon on stand-by over the weekend, should surgery be necessary. A vascular radiologist did an ultrasound of the wound, which showed that there was a "false aneurysm" under the site oozing quite a large flow of blood.

The team of doctors had decided to put pressure on the wound to try and force the blood in the false aneurysm sac to dissipate. According to protocol, this procedure should only be performed on small aneurysms. However, they felt they had no option but to proceed due to Jack's high risk of stroke and heart failure. A large, heavy clamp was applied to the site. They made it clear to me that they wanted to spare Jack any surgery. At this point they were still denying that the infection could have originated at the site. After repeated checks on Jack, they left him like that for over 3 hours.

On Saturday, Jack was delirious again and his right leg began to swell from the site downward gradually until it was quite swollen by evening. After the cardiovascular surgeon examined him, he was finally transferred from Emergency to a room. The resident who had performed the angiogram dropped in to see us. He was now working in another hospital in the district, but had kept abreast of Jack's case. As he was not present at the ultrasound done the previous evening, he took Jack down and carried out another one himself. He subsequently scheduled him to be seen by a vascular specialist in order to rule out possible blood clots in the right leg, and was gone as suddenly as he had come in. It was obvious that he was concerned, and I acknowledged my appreciation. The Doppler test subsequently confirmed there were no blood clots in the leg.

On Sunday, Jack did not look well at all when we arrived after church. The nurse informed us that his blood pressure was low and that the operation would take place that afternoon. Right then the surgeon called in to talk to me; however, when the nurse gave him the latest blood pressure reading, he decided against the operation.

Monday, September 13th, the neuroradiologist called me into his office. He explained that, although after the extra 2 days of antibiotics Jack was more stable, he still feared that surgery would be detrimental to him. For that reason they had decided to do a vascular angiogram from the opposite (left) side. This would entail pushing a balloon-tipped device against the site in order to push the blood out and simultaneously inserting a coagulant to stop the blood flow and seal the femoral arterial aneurysm.

During this procedure I witnessed an aide coming and going at least 3 times to get another balloon-tipped device from across the hall. It was later confirmed that they had to gradually insert bigger "balloons" as the smaller ones did not suffice. After that Jack was left for about an hour for observation to see whether the now sizeable swelling would subside, while I kept on praying. It did not.

The vascular surgeon was finally summoned; by now it was after 6 p.m. He charged into the room to meet his new patient, obviously very upset about the fact that he had not been consulted regarding all the previous decisions. As he was not on duty during the weekend, he did not know anything about Jack's condition. Having to instantly take over as the attending doctor, his major concern was that now it had become an emergency situation with no time to waste. He felt terrible that he would not be able to perform the operation before evening the next day as he was already fully booked. In the meantime an echocardiogram, or ultrasound of the heart, was ordered to determine the exact status of Jack's heart.

The ultrasound detected defective valves as well as an enlarged ventricle; signs of previous heart failure. The next day Jack was taken down to Surgery around 4, and it was suggested that I go for a long walk and not return before 5. He was wheeled out of the O.R. at 7:30. When I met with the surgeon, he was visibly exhausted. He acknowledged fatigue, adding that usually he was never tired after an operation, but this one had been difficult. The vein had to be patched and he did not think he would succeed. I thanked him very much and assured him that Jack would pull through. Giving me a quizzical look, he turned and walked off. After about an hour in the recovery room Jack was transferred to an isolation room in the intermediate I.C.U.

A couple of days later Jack was transferred to an isolation room on the floor because of the Staphylococci infection. We were happy that we had the privacy of the room, even though it meant donning a yellow gown and gloves before entering. His leg remained swollen and I was told repeatedly by the surgeon that this swelling would remain forever. I asserted that it would go down and be totally healed. Within a week the swelling went down to about half. The healing process over the next several weeks went up and down due to several careless mistakes by the night staff, causing another infection in the wound.

30. Rehabilitation?

Around the last week of September Jack was starting to do better and the leg condition had abated again. He started doing minor physiotherapy in bed, mainly evaluation, and was told to do some arm exercises during his own time. After a couple of weeks the physiotherapist arranged to take him down to the department to be evaluated for sitting and/or standing. Up until now the only way they could get him up was with an electric lift where he would be strapped into a kind of hammock and then very gingerly lowered into a chair. He could not move his right leg and minimum pressure was to be applied to it until it was fully healed. Although the wound had been steadily improving, I was surprised about the sudden decision. However, I mused, if it was ordered, then it was a good sign that there was significant improvement. I kept walking in hope and faith.

It must be noted here that we were now in a French hospital. In Montreal, Quebec, Canada, where we live, the official language is French. English is second. The Quebec Labour law states that every job requires fluency in French, even in predominantly English companies serving anglophone clients. In the English-speaking hospitals and social service organizations all personnel are required to be well versed in English and be fluent in French. Now in this completely French milieu, although there were quite a few English patients, they were not required to serve in English; consequently most of the personnel spoke only French.

I am blessed to have a good command of the French language, but Jack is not. Besides, when talking medical terminology, which even in one's own mother tongue is a challenge, it was very hard to make myself understood even about Jack's daily needs. There were also many household words I did not know, which you don't learn in textbooks! Jack was totally in the dark without me by his side trying to explain every word that was said about him and his condition. It was frustrating to say the least. The nurse assigned to Jack in this isolation room was exceptionally efficient and kind, but she could only communicate in French. All the doctors, however, spoke to us in perfect English.

On Wednesday the 6th, I went down with him to physio and asked the orderlies why he was being transported on a stretcher instead of the customary wheelchair he sat in for a while every day. The response was that he was ordered to go on a stretcher. At Physio they made him get up and then ordered him to stand! This was a major challenge for him; he was literally doubled over in pain, and told them so. "How can they go from one extreme to another!" I gasped in disbelief. His muscles had not been used at all for a long time! He was subsequently ordered to walk between the parallel bars! They had asked me to remain at the entrance of this big gym; they were at the far end, and had made it very clear that they were the professionals and they had a mandate.

I was stunned and could not believe my eyes! This did not seem to be a gradual progression from practically no exercise in bed to this. Before I could get a word out (I felt like screaming but nothing came) Jack, supported on each side by an attendant, walked as fast as he could to the end of the bars and back again. I felt helpless, confused and very, very frustrated. He was returned to his room on the stretcher shortly thereafter. I did not know what to say or think. All I could do was pray.

Remembering how gradually the physio team at the General had worked with Jack after being 1 month in I.C.U., it seemed that here every department was autonomous. Yet, each time Jack left to go anywhere, his voluminous file went with him, Physio being no exception. Had everyone in question taken the time to read it, I wondered. This physio had come to see Jack for over 2 weeks in his room and had been given strict instructions not to have him do anything strenuous. Anyway, I did assume that the doctor had given the O.K., so I focused on standing in faith and asked the

Lord to turn it into a positive outcome. After all, he did walk and I was looking forward to a quick, remarkable recovery.

31. The Consequences

The next morning I got a call around 8. from Jack's nurse stating that there had been much bleeding during the night and that the doctor would be in later to decide what to do. By the time I arrived, Jack looked grey and suddenly mumbled: "What do I do now?" Wheeling around as I was donning my yellow gown and gloves, I noticed that he was nauseous and there was blood on the blanket. I instantly rang the bell, and the nurse came running. Praise God for her efficiency! She immediately summoned all the residents and doctors, who happened to be in the conference room across the hall, to stem the blood as she ran to call the surgeon. Jack was rushed to the O.R., and a by-pass operation was performed immediately (literally within 15 minutes). There was a tear between the artery and the vein at the spot of the previous operation. Jack was kept in surgical I.C.U. overnight.

The next morning I woke up very early and had a premonition to go to the hospital earlier than usual. As I got there around 8, I saw a number of doctors all around Jack but I was not allowed into his room. I was told that he had suddenly lost 50% of his blood within 5 seconds, and that they could do nothing but tie the blood vessels. As they rushed him past me to the O.R., I noticed one doctor literally sitting on top of him pushing down on the wound with all his might to keep the blood from spurting out. I touched Jack's head and told him to hang on; that I knew he would be O.K. They all turned around, looking at me in disbelief as if to say: "Lady, you don't know what you are talking about!" The vascular surgeon explained briefly that the only way to stop the bleeding was to tie all the blood supply to the right leg, adding that he did not expect him to make it through the procedure.

The first call went out to our pastor. I knew that he was an early bird; he assured me he would be over right away. He had continued to visit, and pray for, Jack on a regularly basis. Within half an hour he was there as well as Annie, whom he had summoned on the way. I burst into tears when I saw her, being touched by her immediate response and love. We prayed powerfully and fervently in the spirit; I felt completely at peace. As people from time to time opened the waiting room door, they silently retreated as they noticed the prayer going on.

At 9:30 with the family gathered together, the doctor came to tell us that Jack was back and that he had tied the blood supply to and from his right leg. I thanked him and acknowledged that Jack had survived, despite his prognosis. His answer was: "We'll see!"

Where there is prayer and faith, the enemy will come in to try and curb the faith so he can have the victory. We were all wise to the devil's tactics and we stood even more steadily in our faith, fully understanding at the same time that, from the physician's point of view, Jack's chances of survival were nil.

32. At Death's Door

The doctor returned a few minutes later with a resident and sat down with us to give a complete overview of the situation. Jack was on total life support and there was not much more they could do from a medical standpoint. Enquiring what "not much more" referred to, he answered: "Amputation." I flinched. He added that such a procedure was done maybe once in twenty years and that because Jack's heart that morning was less than 15% capacity, his kidneys were not functioning at all, and his blood pressure was extremely low, his recommendation was to "just let him die in peace."

We asked if we could consult together as a family for a few minutes. His answer was: "Yes, I was doing something upstairs; I have to go there for a few minutes; I'll be back." We consulted some more with the resident doctor who confirmed that, despite the stress factors on the body, amputation would give Jack the only hope medically available. He told us that of all the I.C.U. patients, Jack was "the sickest one of all."

We all went to fervent prayer again; this time asking the Lord specifically for his wisdom and divine Will in this situation. As Christians, we all knew that Jack loved the Lord and would have eternal life with him. We were not afraid of dying nor worried about Jack's going to be with his Lord. That was not an issue at all. I had been praying for long life for Jack, and the Lord had given him life. Now, a year later, we did not believe that was all that the Lord wanted for Jack! I was by now very aware of the fact that numerous mistakes had been made, but I also knew my God.

"For we have not an high priest which cannot be touched with the feeling of our infirmities; but was in all points

tempted like as we are, yet without sin. Let us therefore come boldly unto the throne of grace, that we may obtain mercy, and find grace to help in time of need. "[32]

All of us recognized and acknowledged the satanic opposition throughout Jack's recuperative ordeal. It had not been easy. I again asked for forgiveness from the Lord where I might not have clearly heard his Will regarding the second angiogram. I had listened to my flesh (mind as opposed to spirit), where I now realized I should have gone to my pastor and others for concerted prayer and godly advice. This may have opened a door to the devil, who would thereby have a right to enter and play around with Jack's health.

---

[32] Heb. 4:15,16

33. But God!

It is not God who causes sickness; it is always his Will that his children suffer no harm. But, in order to achieve that, we must walk closely with him day by day, obey his commandments, read his Word, and walk in faith. It is so important to know him. We cannot have salvation, healing, or any of our needs met through our own will. However, when we submit to God with a humble and contrite heart filled with faith and love for him, his Holy Spirit can, and will, perform miracles.

"He that is hanged is accursed of God"[33]

"I have power to lay it down"[34]

"As many were astonished at thee; his visage was so marred more than any man, and his form more than the sons of man. So shall he sprinkle many nations; the kings shall shut their mouths at him : for that which had not been told them shall they see; and that which they had not heard shall they consider."[35]

"...he hath no form of comeliness; and when we shall see him, there is no beauty that we should desire him"[36]

"Surely he hath borne our griefs (sickness) and carried our sorrows (weakness/pain); yet we did esteem him

---

[33] Deut. 21:23
[34] John 10 :18
[35] Isa. 52 :14,15
[36] Isa. 53 : 2

stricken, smitten of God, and afflicted. But he was wounded for our transgressions, he was bruised for our iniquities (sins); the chastisement of our peace was upon him; and with his stripes we are healed. All we like sheep have gone astray; we have turned every one to his own way; and the Lord hath laid on him the iniquity of us all. He was oppressed, and he was afflicted, yet he opened not his mouth: he is brought as a lamb to the slaughter, and as a sheep before her shearers is dumb, so he openeth not his mouth..Yet it pleased the Lord to bruise him; he hath put him to grief: when thou shalt make his soul an offering for sin, he shall see his seed, he shall prolong his days...He...shall justify many; for he shall bear their iniquities "[37]

This, in a nutshell, is the whole gospel prophesied before Jesus Christ was born. The whole reason God came to earth in the form of a man was to lay down his life and willingly become a curse for us. But the good news is that he did not stay on that cross!

When I think of how he bore those stripes for my healing, I cannot fathom it. The picture of him hanging on the cross, disfigured more than any man, and that God had put on him the iniquity of us all! I cannot begin to imagine that, aside from beatings, scourgings and thorns he endured, he bore all the sins of mankind and all the sicknesses there ever would be! There is nothing left out. Of course, there is no way he does not intend to heal anyone of anything! He has already done it, once and for all! And all we have to do is believe it, accept it, and thank and praise him for it!

Having had Jack home coherent and relatively well for 3 months I knew that he had the will to live, and he had the faith. His family was everything to him and he knew that the Lord had much for him to do, not the least of which was being a father and mentor to Sergio. Furthermore, Mark was starting up a business and he was eager to be involved with that. And for those very reasons it

---

[37] Isa. 53: 4-11

had meant so much to him to get his mind back in order to function properly. He was a fighter, and he would expect nothing less from us on his behalf now. Peace was over all of us and after the prayer we were unanimous in our decision to "go for life" and give Jack a chance.

34. A Life for a Limb

As by 3:30 the surgeon had still not returned, we asked to have him paged. His answer to the nurse was: "I'll be there at 5:30." The strange thing was that during all those hours of praying, singing, and encouraging Jack, time had gone in a flash and we were in total peace. When the doctor finally arrived together with the resident, he told us that he had consulted with sixty-one other medical doctors, who had all agreed with him that amputation for a patient in Jack's present condition was considered "over-procedure." The resident this time was in agreement with him. They obviously had been anticipating the patient's imminent death all day!

But Jack held on as we kept him soaked in prayer and words of encouragement. The verse that kept coming in my spirit to pray over him was:

"If the same Spirit that raised up Jesus from the dead dwell in you, he that raised up Christ from the dead shall also quicken (make alive) your mortal bodies by his Spirit that dwelleth in you"[38]

We adamantly held to our decision. The surgeon finally agreed, saying that he would honour the patient's family's decision to amputate. However, since it was "over-procedure," I would have to sign a consent form authorizing that in the event of heart failure, there would be no attempt at resuscitation. As well, the hospital under these circumstances would not administer kidney dialysis,

---

[38] Rom. 8:11

which would be urgently required by morning due to the complete shutdown of his renal functions.

The amputation finally took place at 7:30 that evening. Jack returned to I.C.U. at 9:30. "Praise God!" we exclaimed in unison. The surgeon countered that, if he were to survive the next day and taking into account his low immune system, infections would set in. This would necessitate surgical trimming. We ignored the negative reports; we were happy that day was over! The surgeon had been used by God, and our Jack wàs going to live! And that was all we were focusing on at that moment.

During the amputation I called Wilf. We had decided to wait until we had something concrete to tell them. I was in tears at that point, asking them forgiveness for having brought Jack back to the hospital. Wilf immediately decided that he would drive over the next day, which happened to be Sue's birthday and the Canadian Thanksgiving weekend.

As one by one we went to see Jack after he was settled back into his room, I did not want to look at the leg. Then, gingerly glancing over, my immediate reaction was nausea. It was awful and to realize this had been his good leg! I took a hold of myself and we buoyed each other up before retiring for the night to our respective homes. The recurring verse that kept ringing in my mind was: "I shall yet praise him!"[39] I said it out loud over and over again, and proceeded to praise the Lord. I knew that was the answer and I felt so good as I did it! God deserves the praise for his greatness and majesty, regardless of our circumstances. And, while we praise him, our circumstances and moods change. I knew that I knew that Jack was going to be fine!

As I reached the elevator, there stood Jack's neurosurgeon. We had not seen him at all in this hospital. Jack was not under his care; yet I knew that, working in liaison with the neuroradiologist, he would have kept up-to-date on the situation. His head was down. I instantly knew that he was aware of everything that had

---

[39] Ps. 42:11

just transpired. He acknowledged feeling bad; but could find no words to express himself.

Thanksgiving Saturday morning, October 9th, I called I.C.U. from home at 6:30. "No change; please call again around 9:30." I did not panic; I was sure all along that he would pull through. I called again on my way out the door; still no appreciable change. As I entered around 10, I was told that his blood pressure was steadily rising, his kidneys were working perfectly, and his heart was stable!

They had no explanation for the kidneys other than there must have been a blockage in the catheter drain! I had personally checked that, having become acutely aware of medical procedures over the many months with Jack in hospital. "Surely they had checked the Creatinine level in the blood samples taken throughout the day," I mused. I knew that this was a routine procedure and definitive proof of the state of the kidneys, but said nothing. They could not understand miraculous intervention, and somehow had to explain it away. It did not matter! My Jack would make it!

As we all gathered that morning, our faith levels were soaring. We notified Pastor Frey and others and asked them to keep standing with us in prayer. Liv and Val, who had gone to meet Wilf outside, jubilantly returned with him exactly at noon, as he had promised. He was visibly relieved about Jack's progress and sheepishly admitted that he had called Sue halfway between Toronto and Montreal to see if she had any further reports, fearing the worst.

In the afternoon Kaz and Betty arrived with oodles of fruit and nutritious goodies. It was a time of fellowship as we took turns comforting Jack. That evening Wilf got a taste of Sergio's culinary expertise and their hospitality. We feasted on a meal fit for a king and had a wonderful time of celebration. Sunday morning the congregation surrounded us all with prayer and thanked God for His miraculous intervention. It was a wonderful time of praise and thanksgiving.

In saying farewell to Wilf, I assured him that Jack was healed. He instantly acknowledged it, saying: "You know, when I spoke with the doctor, he told me to prepare myself for the worst; that Jack had no chance of survival. But I told the doctor that with the powerhouse of prayer behind him, Jack was going to live!" He went home with his faith level lifted high. He, too, learned that our Lord is in the healing business and had turned our sorrow into dancing!

35. No Easy Ride

The surgeon admitted being very surprised about the results. He asked: "How will Mr. Stewart react when he realizes he has lost a leg?" I answered that he would not like it initially but that, being the man he is, he would be happy to be alive and thankful for the difficult decision we had to make on his behalf. He answered: "O.K.," displaying a sense of relief as he obviously was concerned about the patient. Even Jack's nurse before the amputation had told me: "Madame, you should think about the patient."

Amputation seemed "taboo" to them. When we enquired about the pros and cons of amputation the previous day, the doctor had admitted that he did not have a lot of expertise in that field. I am sure it was a gutsy thing for him to do. I affirmed how much I appreciated him going through with it, and that I would break the news to Jack that very day.

Being on a high dose of sedatives and antibiotics, I was not sure how much Jack heard or understood, but I told him as gently as I could what had transpired. Once slowly weaned off the respirator a few days later, he whispered something to me. As I leaned over to hear him better, he repeated: "Where is my leg?" I told him that he had been at death's door and it was the only option open for his life. He whispered: "I know!" Wondering what he meant, he answered my thoughts, saying: "I knew right away; I could feel it." I was glad that I had told him the previous week, even though I didn't think he had understood. He seemed to be taking it matter-of-factly.[vi]

The nurse exclaimed: "Madame, I wish I had faith like you!" At first puzzled by her exclamation, wondering how she knew, I realized that she had witnessed our praying, tape-playing and calm determination during this time of stress. We sure had prayed up a storm in that tiny waiting room, not being exactly quiet about it! I gave the Lord the praise and wished I could have had more time with her to share his goodness and love. However, she was constantly on the go between patients and could only communicate in French. However, seeds had been sown, and I have since kept her in my prayers. She was excellent and had great empathy for Jack.[vii]

The neuroradiologist also went out of his way to come and see us. He acknowledged that, after consultation with his team, they had agreed that a revision of the angiogram procedure would be carefully considered, even though it was beneficial to the majority of their patients.

Jack contracted E.coli (Gram-negative) and consequently was kept in isolation in I.C.U. Val cringed when she heard it, but at that time I was not aware of the gravity of this disease and did not want to know anything about it then! Prayer continued to be the order of the day. About a week later a mild form of chickenpox was added to Jack's misery.

The week after Thanksgiving an evangelist by the name of Tallat Mohamed and his wife Anne, were visitors at our Wednesday evening church service. Tallat gave a testimony of what the Lord had done in his life. As an abandoned Muslim child in Guyana the Lord had taken him out of the slums, and now his whole mission in life is to preach the gospel. Through his evangelistic outreach, Regions Beyond Evangelism, he ministers all over the world. He related how he has witnessed many recreative miracles, including full legs growing on amputees as well as arms and feet where there were none!

Tallat did not know anything about Jack's condition. They were personal friends of Bernard and Michele in our church, who had invited them. This was God's doing; His perfect timing! I asked them if they would be in town the next day and, if so, would they come to the hospital and pray over Jack? Immediately Tallat and Anne agreed, and Bernard and Michele offered to bring them.

36. For Such a Time As This

This was the sixth day after Jack's death's door experience. Beside his bed I placed a brown paper bag with his clothes and a pair of shoes. My mind was telling me: "Ann, you're crazy" but my spirit said:

> *"Whosoever shall confess that Jesus is the Son of God, God dwelleth in him, and he in God"*[40]

> *"For whatsoever is born of God overcometh the world; and this is the victory that overcometh the world, even our faith"*[41]

> *"Is any sick among you? ...And the prayer of faith shall save the sick, and the Lord shall raise him up... "*[42]

> *"And this is the confidence that we have in him, that, if we ask any thing according to his will, he heareth us: And if we know that he hear us, whatsoever we ask, we know that we have the petitions that we desired of him"*[43]

I believed, and I knew that this man of God was sent here "for such a time as this."

Tallat and I went to pray over Jack in the tiny I.C.U. chamber; the others were praying in the waiting room. Realizing the gravity of the patient's condition, he asked if I had the faith at that moment

---

[40] 1 John 4:15
[41] 1 John 5:4
[42] Jas. 5:14-15
[43] 1 John 5:14-15

for a recreative miracle. I responded in the affirmative. He explained that this kind of miracle usually happens whenever there is a lot of combined faith and expectation by thousands of people gathered together praising God in unison. My mouth dropped momentarily but I was instantly reminded of how I personally had received healings, as did Jack, and that we had seen miracles before our very eyes. This would be just another touch from my Lord.

My God is not only able, but to him healing a headache is no different than recreating a limb! So, we prayed. The first thing he prayed was that, if the same Spirit that raised Christ from the dead reside in Jack, then he will raise him! What an immediate confirmation to me! The little room was charged with the presence of God. Nothing visibly happened. We then joined the group and continued in prayer with them for some time. I took Jack's clothes back home but continued in faith. It's done; it's going to happen – in his time!

Months later Jack told me that during his time in I.C.U. he had heard the Lord say: "The same Spirit that rose me from the dead dwells in you. Look; I got the keys; now get up!" He hung onto these words throughout his recuperation.

37. Careful for Nothing

On October 25 Jack was about to be returned to his regular room when blood results indicated a bowel infection referred to as E.R.V., or: Enteritis Resistant to Vancomycin. This was the so-called wonder drug; in other words, if that does not cure it, nothing will.

Jack was subsequently transferred to the isolation wing on the top floor set aside for highly contagious cases. There he also had his own room and everyone had to go through the yellow gown and gloves routine again.

Now Jack went down to the Physio Department every morning where he was lowered with a lift into a warm antiseptic whirlpool bath for thorough cleansing of the wound, soothing the pain, and promoting faster healing. It was very stressful for Jack, who would have preferred to stay quietly in bed.

Recurring nightmares plagued me about the "if onlys," i.e. "If only I could put the clock back," "if only Jack had not had the angiogram," "if only time had not been lost regarding the infection," … the list went on and on!

Ultimately I had blamed myself but I had asked and received forgiveness for not having listened more closely to the Lord, and he had forgiven me. I also took immediate control of my mind every time those thoughts would come to the forefront, which happened mostly at night. I refused to entertain any negative thoughts. The Bible says that we have control of our thoughts:

"..Casting down imaginations, and every high thing that exalteth itself against the knowledge of God, and bringing into captivity every thought to the obedience of Christ "[44]

The Lord kept reminding me:

"Be careful for nothing; but in every thing by prayer and supplication with thanksgiving let your requests be made known unto God. And the peace of God, which passeth all understanding, shall keep your hearts and minds through Christ Jesus. Finally, whatsoever things are true, whatsoever things are just, whatsoever things are lovely, whatsoever things are of good report; if there be any virtue, and if there be any praise, think on these things. "[45]

So, I did!

---

[44] 2 Cor. 10:5
[45] Phil. 4:6-8

38. Trials and Tribulations

The following week Jack displayed a severe reaction to a sudden change in medication. One day I was told he had vomited continually most of the morning and would not eat. That morning when the nurse asked him if he was in pain, she took it upon herself to administer meds that had been prescribed during his I.C.U. stay. He had since been on a much milder analgesic. I suggested that the discomfort he now had was not to be compared with the acute pain back then, and that most likely this medicine was the cause of his present discomfort. Jack acknowledged this. However, the nurse snubbed the idea, and continued giving it to him whenever she had to dress the wound. Finally, on the third day of nausea and no sustenance, the doctor stopped the drug immediately when he noticed the results. The nurse had not paged to consult with him during that whole time.

Another day the same nurse told me that it was written on the file that, if Jack's heart should fail, they were not to resuscitate him! At that moment I appreciated the fact that this was said in French as we were standing at Jack's bedside. In as calm a voice as I could muster, anger seething up on the inside, I explained to her that the form in question, signed by me, had applied to the amputation procedure only and was no longer in force. She countered that the doctor should subsequently have rescinded it, and that I would have to take it up with him because: "You know, madame, after all in fatal cases…"

I did not see the surgeon again for 2 days. Since Jack was no longer in danger, he did not make his rounds as often. On the third day, staying later than usual in the hope of seeing him, I found out inadvertently from the evening nurse that the note not to resuscitate had already been rescinded on the file! The doctor had made the

115

entry on the same day the query had come up. I was relieved that this was done, but could not understand why the nurse would withhold such vital information from the family, knowing that I did not want to miss the doctor for that very reason.

39. Waiting and Watching

On November 4th the plastic surgeons grafted skin taken from Jack's upper right leg to close the wound just below it. We were so happy that he was on the mend now. There had been no sign of the contagious Enteritis, Praise God! As well, the dreaded Staphylococci also seemed to be gone! However, nothing had been said to confirm or deny either infection, and we were still wearing the gowns. Meanwhile, we were happy to have our own private wing. We played praise music to our hearts' content, not having to put the volume down to where you could hardly hear it. This made it a much more uplifting atmosphere.

There were 2 to 3 other patients at the most at any one time on that whole wing. Jack and I would go up and down the long corridor, sit together in the sunshine at the very end, and I was even allowed the use of the staff room to brew a cup of tea or coffee. Furthermore, it was very quiet and, most importantly, it kept Jack safe from attracting more "bugs" to himself.

This time Jack was ordered to have more aggressive physiotherapy to strengthen primarily the atrophying muscles on the amputated leg as fast as possible. Without that Jack would be plagued with phantom leg syndrome, i.e. feeling the whole leg as if it were still there!

The physiotherapist this time was fluently bilingual and very capable. In order to firm up the muscles, she had to push down quite forcibly onto the leg, right where they had scraped the skin for the graft. Gingerly testing different spots, all the while asking Jack if it hurt, she determined the approximate area, as the whole area was bandaged. When I asked if that part of the physio could be postponed until it had healed, she explained that she had to follow orders and that it was crucial for Jack's recuperation and rehabilitation. I then realized from the Montreal General experience that they were on a mandate to push patients out, either home, to rehab, or to a nursing home. His acute care treatment was coming to an end.

This went on for a couple of days, with me critically watching where she pushed with all her might onto the graft site. Jack did not flinch but I knew that most of the whole upper surface was very sensitive. She assured me that by applying the flat hand it would not get damaged. However, when the plastic surgeons came to evaluate the healing, they were surprised to note that the site was still extremely tender and had not yet started to scab. Finally the physio regime was altered somewhat. The blood thinner no doubt contributed to the delayed healing and sensitive nature of the graft.

The healing process went slowly but my guy did well in physio, gradually progressing from exercising leg and arm muscles to hopping between the bars. No, he was not yet the happy-go-lucky Jack we used to know, but he was motivated to get out of there.

40. Happy Birthday, Jack!

For his birthday on Saturday, December 4th, I asked the social worker whether Jack could go home for the day. She thought it would be an excellent idea to re-introduce him to life outside the hospital and to spend some quality time with the family. The nurse ordered special wheelchair transportation 2 days in advance to pick him up early in the morning and return him after supper. This was wonderful. We all celebrated together and, although it was tiresome for Jack, it was a miracle breakthrough.

The following Saturday Wilf was in town and we arranged the same. This was a wonderful, emotional reunion for the two brothers, finally seeing each other for the first time that Jack was not in I.C.U.! From then on he came home every Saturday.

For Christmas Jack was ready to come for the whole weekend. It was pre-arranged for an orderly to come every day to bathe him, as well as a nurse to dress the wound. He was to be picked up at 4 o'clock at the hospital. I stayed with him at the nurses' station until about 4:30. Due to traffic and/or double booking it was always hard for the bus to be exactly on time. We agreed that by the time I got to the car, taking into consideration the rush hour and a snowstorm, I would go ahead so that I would be home before his arrival.

I had supper all prepared, went out to shovel the driveway 3 times so that the wheelchair had no trouble getting through and over the ramps, but still no Jack! Before leaving the hospital I had asked the nurse to check the status of the bus to be sure they were on their way. She stated tersely that protocol required to order the transportation 2 days in advance, which she had done. Around 6 I called, only to find out that Jack had just left, having sat at the nurses' station the whole time with his winter coat on. The head nurse had finally called the company just before the end of her shift. There had been a glitch and Jack had been overlooked.

Jack was not used to sitting up for long periods of time; so by the time he came home he was exhausted. "But," he remarked, "it was great driving through the snow and to see all the familiar sights again!" That was my Jack! He was coming back!

41. On the Way Back!

Finally, on the 2nd day of February we triumphantly left the hospital en route to a rehabilitation facility. As we left the isolation wing we were told that they were closing it; Jack was their last patient.

As we got off the elevator at the rehab, there waiting for us was Richard, a former neighbour who had lived across the street from us! He was in for a broken hip and was to be Jack's roommate for the next couple of weeks. There was a sunroom with a television and large round table where Jack and I would have our lunch while watching the noon-hour news. All in all Jack started to blossom there; his appetite was good and he did well in his therapies. The evaluation team ascertained that he was not a candidate for a prosthesis, mainly because of his heart condition. As well, the wound was still tender, the amputation high, and his left leg was still not responding 100% due to some nerve damage.

This particular facility's main thrust was amputees. It was not pleasant to see so many people with limbs missing, but it made Jack realize that his case was indeed not rare. One morning we were invited to a support group on the premises where rehabilitated amputees shared how they were coping alone. It was very informative and good to hear the positive outcomes in these people's lives. Most had lost their limbs due to Diabetes. One lady shared that she was so happy she had made the choice as it was far better for her than the excruciating pain she had before the operation. It was a positive eye opener and faith builder for Jack. After all, if they could do it, then with the Lord on his side, he could definitely do it. I reminded him of his favourite scripture verse:

"I can do all things through Christ which strengtheneth me."[46]

He smiled and gave me the thumbs up sign!

Jack related very well to the physio- and occupational therapists. They were both exceptional and very patient, teaching him specific exercises of how to transfer smoothly from a bed onto a wheelchair and vice versa, and how to propel his wheelchair. It was difficult to do the exercises, taking his heart and stamina into consideration. Jack had never been physically strong and now, after the wasting away of the muscles for such a long time, it was still an uphill battle. Up until his last hospitalization he had used his feet to propel his wheelchair. This time he had to use his arms, which meant more strain on the heart. Whereas in the hospital the focus had been on strengthening the leg and arm muscles, now they concentrated on the specifics of becoming as independent as possible in the home environment.

As had become his custom at the hospital, Jack was encouraged to continue his weekend visits home. He was taught how to slide in and out of the car on a smooth wooden transfer board. They actually had a cut-off front end of a car, which they used for practice. That was really neat, as we did not have to go out to practice in the arctic February weather. Jack was now able to go home with me right after the afternoon occupational therapy session on Fridays around 3 and return Sunday evenings. I was so happy that he was now only about 20 minutes away from home as compared to almost an hour's trek to the hospital. I was always there for his physio at 9, and would usually stay until after his supper.

All throughout Jack's various hospital stays I had missed only 2 days; one the day after I fainted at the General, the other that dismal day of sleet when Deane and I picked up the car. All during the long ordeal I did not even get so much as a cold! "Oh Lord,

---

[46] Phil.4:13

you're good!" It's only in the looking back on our lives that we come to realize and appreciate how the hand of the Lord has sustained us!

As the snow began to melt in the March sun I would take Jack out for walks around the premises and gradually across the street to a small shopping centre for a favourite treat: pecan pie or butter tart and a ginger ale! As his taste buds improved, so did his spirits. On his weekends home we would take a drive and/or visit the local shopping mall. His eyes became bright and his talk more animated. Now he knew he was on the road to recovery and the final homecoming was but a matter of weeks away.

42. Home to Stay

Finally, April 2nd, 2000 was here; the day of his homecoming!
He was ready! His leg had healed well but now we needed some
more adaptations for his optimal functioning in the house, such as
a vertical floor-to-ceiling pole with a horizontal bar to pull himself
up in order to swivel onto bed or chair. This time I requested a
female orderly, considering their innate motherly expertise and
sense of hygiene.

Jack now had a permit to travel on specially adapted city buses
or taxis, and soon was enrolled in a weekly computer course at a
rehabilitation centre for outpatients. He enjoyed the ride into town
and back, and would even give the driver directions. One snowy
evening, arriving over an hour late, he was jubilant. He explained
that the driver had skirted the main arteries in the storm and
dropped off the other passengers first. He thoroughly enjoyed
going through a lot of old, familiar territory; to him it was a sheer
treat.

43. I Will Hasten My Word to Perform It

It is so crucial to have a close relationship with the Lord. In the quiet times with him he talks and he leads. In early summer of 1998 just before Jack's aneurysm he had led us to attend a weeklong conference with a visiting evangelist. That man of God prophesied over Liv and the family in essence that it was time to stop sitting and to start doing. Pow! Right from the heart of God. It confirmed exactly what we had been feeling and sharing with each other!

We were all hungry for more growth in the Word of Faith. When Jack and I prayed for direction, the Lord opened up the first page of Jeremiah to us and there, staring at us was:

"I will hasten my word to perform it"[47]

Jack and I continued silently in prayer, and did not talk about it to anyone. What Liv decided was between her and the Lord. Deane was not present at that particular meeting. The next Sunday night we were fast asleep in bed when I heard Deane come home. She had been out with Mark; it must have been around midnight. She was so excited. I heard her whisper at our bedroom door, in the hope that I was still awake yet not to disturb her dad. I groggily got up to see what the enthusiasm was all about.

There on the kitchen table lay a number of pamphlets. "Oh mom," she said, "you've got to come and see. At lunch after church Mark and I got to talking with Kaz and Betty that we feel a

---

[47] Jer. 1:12

nudging from the Holy Spirit that it's time to move on. We don't know why or where, but one thing led to another and all 4 of us decided to attend the evening service at this new church in town." She continued that when they had attended a conference there earlier that year, she had felt so at home there.

She related how they had been warmly received, and instantly wanted to join the vibrant group for young adults, something that, due to the size of our church, had been lacking in their lives. By now Liv also joined the little group and was caught up by her sister's contagious enthusiasm. She interjected that Sergio had also sought out that church recently and that they, too, had been considering joining that group!

This was a church that was strong in the Word of Faith. Not known to either of the girls was Jack's strong desire to be in a ministry outreach for and by seniors. He had a recurring vision of an eagle with its wings outspread. Here on the table in front of me was a pamphlet with a beautiful eagle in full flight! Upon closer examination, I read that it was a ministry for people over sixty, led by Annie.

Now I could not be contained. I had to tell Jack. Of course, with all that commotion, who could sleep? He had heard the whole conversation. In typical Jack fashion he replied: "That's good," then rolled over and went back to sleep. The next morning he woke me up early and said that during the night (he hears from the Lord in the quiet of the night) he had a vivid vision of us sitting in that particular church, and that the following Sunday we would go there.

How the Lord goes before his children! Only he knew that so soon after attending that church Jack and I would be in need of this powerhouse of prayer. The teachings were faith builders in a dimension that we had not heard before. We had loved the churches the Lord had led us to and we had seen many miracles; yet, this one was for "such a time as this." We thought we knew all about faith, but soon found out there was a lot more to learn. The most amazing thing, and a total blessing, was that both girls and their guys also felt the call at the same time. Liv initially did not want to leave a big hole in the music ministry at the church we were attending with Jack, Mark, Deane and her all leaving at once. She was totally committed to it. However, only a few weeks later, due to logistics of carpooling to 2 different churches and visiting Dad in hospital afterwards, she received her release. If ever we had any further doubts about the Lord's leading, that was the final confirmation.

The first thing Jack asked himself out loud as we entered that church was: "I wonder who Annie is?" I pointed to a lovely lady in the front row and suggested: "That may be her; why don't you ask?" He did, and she was! There were hugs as Jack related the Lord's vision of the eagle. It was an instant bonding with that dear sister-in-the-Lord.

Coinciding with Jack's homecoming we were gifted with the most wonderful blessing: a library of cassettes and videos on how to stand in faith from our friends Bernard and Michele. The Lord had called them to the United States. Again, the Lord's perfect timing! From the moment Jack arrived home, we feasted on those cassettes every day, and started speaking Jack's healings and needs out loud. Whenever Jack would complain about something, I would counter: "No! You have been healed," and we would speak a scripture verse over the situation. At first, although Jack had heard the tapes, he would renege, saying that he still had the pain, discomfort, and so on. But, gradually, he started speaking healing scriptures over the situation on his own, loudly and even more forcefully than I had done.

I believe that these teachings have been the major thrust in Jack's continued healing as his mind was being renewed by the Word of God. We both received a deeper revelation of who we are in Christ and what heritage we have in him. This just ignited our faith and hearts. It was impossible to listen to any of those tapes and not feel like dancing in the knowledge that we have the victory!

We became rooted in the knowledge that the New Testament is indeed the Last Will and Testament of Jesus Christ to the Church, which is his Bride. That bride represents everyone who knows him intimately as his or her personal Lord and Saviour. We are his children and he has left us his personal legacy! The Old Testament, although it was first given to the Jewish nation, is now also our inheritance, as we are grafted into the Branch!

> *"...thou, being a wild olive tree (gentile; not the chosen people), wert graffed (or grafted) in among them (Jews), and with them partakest of the root and fatness of the olive tree..."*[48]

> *"...a rod out of the stem of Jesse, and a Branch shall grow out of his roots: and the spirit of the LORD shall rest upon him, the spirit of wisdom and understanding, the spirit of counsel and might, the spirit of knowledge and of the fear of the LORD;"*[49]

So, we know that Jesus is the Branch. To the Jewish nation God bestowed all his blessings, if they would listen to the voice of the Lord and do his commandments.[50] They were under the Law of Moses. However, if they would not do his commandments, they would be cursed:

> *"...every sickness, and every plague, which is not written in the book of this law, them will the Lord bring upon thee..."*[51]

Isn't it wonderful that God provided for each and every kind of sickness that ever would rear its ugly head! It is all our inheritance! However, we are no longer under the Law as:

> *"Christ hath redeemed us from the curse of the law, being made a curse for us: for it is written, Cursed is every one that hangeth on a tree: that the blessing of*

---

[48] Rom. 11:17
[49] Isa. 11:1-2
[50] Deut. 28:1-13
[51] Deut. 28:61

Abraham might come on the gentiles through Jesus Christ; that we might receive the promise of the Spirit through faith.. and if ye be Christ's, then are ye Abraham's seed, and heirs according to the promise. "[52]

"If ye abide in me, and my words abide in you, ye shall ask what ye will, and it shall be done unto you" [53]

"Beloved, if our heart condemn us not, then have we confidence toward God. And whatsoever we ask, we receive of him, because we keep his commandments, and do those things that are pleasing in his sight" [54]

"And this is the confidence that we have in him, that, if we ask any thing according to his will, he heareth us: And if we know that he hear us, whatsoever we ask, we know that we have the petitions that we desired of him" [55]

Oh Lord, we are blessed! By studying his Word, we learn to know his Will, i.e. his express Will is that everyone be healed, anytime, anywhere. Yes, anyone without any reservations, maybes or "who, me?s." If it is the Word of God, then I believe it! And he even gives provision for when we have missed it. He tells us to come humbly with a contrite heart and he will forgive us of all our iniquities. As believers, we are born again, having the Spirit of God residing in us, and we're washed with the blood of Christ:

"...with boldness to enter into the holiest by the blood of Jesus.. Let us draw near with a true heart in full assurance of faith, having our hearts sprinkled from an evil conscience, and our bodies washed with pure water... " [56]

---

[52] Gal. 3:13,14,29
[53] John 15:7
[54] 1 John 3:21-22
[55] 1 John 5:14-15
[56] Heb. 10:19,22

It is one thing to be taught the Word of God; quite another to walk in it. That I found out full well! Especially when everything seems to be going against you and/or your loved one, it's not easy to stand up against all the odds. A lot has to do with the difference between knowing (in your mind) and believing (deep in your heart). That difference only comes with the test of faith. As faith comes by hearing, and hearing by the Word of God, we must constantly be in the Word, confess the Word out loud and pray the Word. Eventually, that Word takes root deep in our hearts. No one and nothing will be able to shake it.

> *"...that ye may be able to withstand in the evil day, and having done all, to stand."*[57]

The standing and waiting is the real test. But, when the results manifest, what glory! And this becomes then your testimony to shout to the whole world: "It's Real! God really does heal, even me! It's really, really true!"

> *"And they overcame him (Satan) by the blood of the Lamb, and by the word of their testimony."*[58]

We must believe it, expect it, and wait in expectation. If we should waver, we can turn to him with a contrite heart, and he'll forgive us and put us back on track.

---

[57] Eph. 6:13
[58] Rev. 12:11

44. I'm Healed!

Jack really took off. He started speaking the Word of God and believing the Bible rather than the circumstances. Soon he became more sociable; he loved to sit in front of the house and watch the world go by. Neighbours would stop to chat; many not having been aware that he had been in hospital all that time. Jack told everyone what the Lord had done. He loved to tell about how he had been left at the brink of death. He explained that he knew from his deathbed that the Lord was healing him, and that had kept him going throughout the lengthy recuperation.

He recognized everyone and knew most by name, yet afterwards he would ask me: "How did I meet that person and what were the circumstances?" He still did not have his short-term memory back and it still bothered him; but this time he did not have the depression any more. Something had lifted in the spirit.

The first Sunday Jack returned to church, he literally lit up during the praise and worship. It was like he suddenly got a shot of Holy Spirit adrenaline! He seemed to realize what he had been missing that past year! Jack also used to be on the worship team and loved to sing praises to his King.

One Sunday morning soon after, in the middle of the praise, I heard Jack shouting: "I'm healed; I'm healed! Can't you see him; he's right there in front of you; I'm healed!" Everyone's eyes were on Jack. Liv, Deane and Mark, on the worship team, had a hard time choking back tears. The music stopped, and Mark was so excited he ran up to Jack. He knew he had a vision from the Lord and wanted to see it, too.

My very first reaction was to check Jack's amputated leg; was it back?? Jack, who noticed my glance, yelled: "No, no; my mind! It's all back! I'm healed!" His memory was the only healing he had asked the Lord for; that was all that mattered to him. "The leg," he said, "that's nothing! I want to be able to function normally; I need my mind!" Everyone was excited for him and Pastor Frey explained that what Jack saw was referred to as an "open vision," which is very rare. It is where the Lord shows up for only one person; no one else can see him. Wow, Jack was no longer downcast! He was totally jubilant. My Jack was back! We all called him "Miracle Jack" from that moment on!

45. The Word of Their Testimony

A week after his healing we got a surprise call from Jack's vascular surgeon, asking: "So, will I see you tomorrow?" I was totally taken aback. Since leaving the hospital Jack had been in rehab for 3 months and home for over a month, and we had not been given a follow-up appointment. He told me that Jack had an appointment at 9 the following morning. I instantly answered that we would be there, secretly thinking: "wait until you see Jack!" Jack, though initially apprehensive about re-entering a hospital, soon got excited about this incredible opportunity to give God the glory right after his miraculous healing!

Mark came with us that morning. It was so precious to see the look on that doctor's face! He hardly said a word; the wheels of his mind must have been spinning overtime. He closed the file (2 huge volumes) and said: "O.K., I can close the file now and send it to Archives." He had kept it open all that time![viii]

Every orderly loved working with Jack, and over the course of a year Jack had become so accustomed to the routine that he would say: "the agency should hire me to train them!" He could not understand why so many of the personnel did not use common sense to be able to adapt to specific needs. Jack had always been big on fundamentals. With the children over the years, whenever they had a problem he would tell them: "go back to your fundamentals." He knew his routine like the back of his hand and no one could mess with his fundamentals; consequently he was dubbed "Fundamental Jack."

During that summer Jack suddenly started getting dizzy spells. After a couple of days I decided to put in a call to the neurosurgeon, fearing it had something to do with the aneurysm. The doctor set my mind at ease when he determined it was due to the heart medication. When I told him that Jack wanted to speak with him, he hesitated a moment as if surprised. Jack calmly yet firmly told him: "You know, doctor, Jesus healed me. He's the best doctor I know!" When Jack handed me back the phone, the surgeon did not hide his surprise as he repeated over and over again: "he sounds so well!" When I told him that Jack was our miracle boy, he answered: "I have no other explanation for it!" The heart medication was promptly adjusted; the dizziness stopped instantly. This was obviously nothing more than an opportunity granted by the Lord to testify to that doctor, who had followed Jack from the very beginning. Up until that moment he had yet to have the opportunity to converse rationally with his patient and get to know the real Jack.[ix]

Every day since his return home we would go for a drive. Now that his mind was "back," we gradually expanded the radius. Everywhere we went, he would shout: "I know that place…that's where so and so…" and he would put his forefinger to his lips, hold it up and defiantly shout: "Chalk up another one, sleuthfoot (his name for the devil); that's another thing they told me I'd never do!"

Our visits went further and further afield. We drove to Laval to get fresh strawberries, and one beautiful summer day we went with Sergio and Liv to Mont Tremblant, a ski and summer resort district. With Sergio pushing Jack through a beautiful nature park, suddenly right in front of us was a beautiful little waterfall. Jack exuberantly yelled: "That's it! That's it, just as the Lord showed me!" He had told me that in a dream recently he had seen a waterfall. The Lord had told him that he had a future for him and that, although man had written him off, he would show him things to come and give him knowledge. Furthermore in that same vision he had asked Jack:

"Whose report do you believe, man's or God's?"[59]

We subsequently went down to Toronto for a weekend and everyone was totally amazed at the wonderful turnaround in Jack's life!

---

[59]   Isaiah 53:1

One of the first things I did since his return home was write a synopsis of Jack's trials and triumphs. I sent these to out-of-town friends, explaining why I had not sent them Christmas cards over the past couple of years. The Lord touched everyone with Jack's testimony and some came over to see us and share past anecdotes. Jack was so happy the visits coincided with his healing. Now he could laugh with the rest of us; he remembered everything!

On December 16, 2000 we celebrated our thirty-fifth wedding anniversary. Suzanne invited the whole family to her place for dinner. We were looking forward to it, and Sergio and Mark would be there to lift Jack up the front steps. It turned out to be a huge surprise party with many friends, some of whom we had not seen for years. Val and Liv had made a huge anniversary card with everyone's best wishes and filled with old snapshots that Liv had supplied. They even arranged a telephone call with my brother John and family from Northern Ontario at just the right moment. It was so wonderful; we did not want it to end. It will stay in our memories forever!

46. Not by Might

In early April 2001 Jack suddenly started having less pep. Everything seemed to demand more of an effort. One evening, sitting in his recliner, he complained that he didn't feel so well and wanted to go to bed. Usually he always looked forward to the evening news but not that day. I barely got him to bed with more effort than usual, and he complained about a strange feeling in his left leg. It was 10 o'clock.

Thoughts raced through my head: 911? Definitely not! I had promised Jack I would never take him into a hospital again! The pastor? But I wanted to know what it was. If it was a stroke, there would be no time to even get him to the hospital. Right away Annie came to mind for 2 reasons: 1) a prayer warrior, and 2) a retired nurse. Immediately I called her, continuing to pray in the Spirit while explaining briefly what was going on. She, too, started praying in the spirit.

Judging by what I described was going on, Annie confirmed my fears: Jack was most likely having a stroke. We just kept right on praying. As I was holding the receiver to Jack's ear for him to hear her prayers, all of a sudden his head arched way back, he became awfully pale, his arms went totally limp, and his eyes went up into their sockets. My head was saying: "He's dead!" Yet I felt completely enveloped in peace and kept right on praying, as did Annie, whom I had kept updated.

Here I was, kneeling on the bed facing him, still holding the phone receiver to his ear. Jack suddenly propelled upright. Staring straight ahead with his hands stretched out in front of him as if pushed by an invisible force, he shouted at the top of his lungs: "I want to stay; I want to stay!" He was totally oblivious of me. Annie was laughing loudly. She instantly knew what had happened. She knew Jack so well; understood his faith, and was there when he received his healing in church. Just as suddenly, Jack relaxed and slumped back onto the pillow. "I saw two hands," he whispered. "I knew they were the Lord's. One was beckoning me to go with him and the other was pushing towards me." He heard the Lord ask him:

"Do you want to come, or do you want to stay? It's your call!"

That's when he instantly responded that he wanted to stay. Jack noted afterwards that he loved how the Lord had used baseball terminology when speaking to him: "It's your call."

Wow! Lord, you did it again! I was laughing and crying at the same time, and so was Annie. There definitely was no doubt in my mind that Jack had the will to live and that the Lord may give us the choice. We're created to fulfill a purpose in the Kingdom of God. He has given everyone talents and tasks to carry out. There is God's Permissive Will, where Jack had a choice to go and be with him forever, but then there is God's Perfect Will. Jack chose to be in his Perfect Will; to walk out here on earth what the Lord has ordained for him.

Jesus with his resurrected body is now at the right hand of the Father. But, he has given us the Holy Spirit, to be our comforter, guide and teacher. We are his body here on earth and, with the help of the Holy Spirit we are equipped to do his work.

"..the Spirit of Truth..ye know him; for he dwelleth in you, and shall be in you..the Comforter, which is the holy Ghost..shall teach you all things" [60]

Within minutes, however, Jack noticed that his left side had "gone." "Where's my left side," he gasped. He had absolutely no feeling all the way down his left side. It was like the only leg he has was not there at all! The next weeks were agony. Everything felt so sensitive; he could only tolerate silky or very soft material

---

[60] John 15:17,26

next to his skin, and transferring into the car or a chair had become a major chore. It took over a month to see a neurologist. We knew that medically there was not much they could do except, hopefully, prescribe something to ease the sensitivity.

Our "happy Jack," who had come from so far and had finally returned with all his humour and joie-de-vivre intact, just the way we had always known him, suddenly "vanished" again. He became grumpy and irritable, and would no longer listen to helpful advice. He was in agony, not being able to feel his foot as he put it down, and having the sense of only being half there.

Even in church, he was only "half there." One Sunday an out-of-town guest at our church, after chatting with us for a few minutes, said that the Lord had put it on her heart to come and pray for Jack. She related how the Lord had healed her from terminal cancer thanks to her father's steadfast faith. He had stayed with her, constantly encouraging her to confess her healing while he also spoke healing scripture verses over her until she was perfectly healed without drugs! Now she is a powerful intercessor in her church and gives her marvelous testimony wherever she goes. We had a wonderful, powerful prayer time together.

One morning a few days later the orderly temporarily left the room. Jack was sitting on the side of the bed with his amputation scars exposed. Out of nowhere, the Lord appeared in front of him! Seeing his nail-pierced hands outstretched towards him, Jack initially looked away, catching his breath, wondering whether to say something to him. Then he slowly turned and said to the Lord: "They did quite a job on you, didn't they?"

The Lord gently leaned over and whispered in his ear: "And you don't look so bad yourself." Then in a very firm voice he added:

"The same Spirit that raised Me from the dead dwells in you. Ann also has the same Spirit. You are not going through this on your own. Ann has told you many times that you will go through this together. Sometimes she may correct you for your own good. The worst is over; from now on it's a piece of cake. Take my hand, I'll lead you through it"

That really shook Jack. He realized that he had been full of self-pity. The Lord also demonstrated to him that, although he had been brutally wounded, he is now glorified and his scars are healed.

It wasn't until some time later that Jack acknowledged to me that the Lord had spoken to him in the way I would sometimes, i.e. in a firm no-nonsense manner. He realized that he had to listen to me; that the Lord used me to get him out of his dilemma, and that sometimes only straight talk would get through; not pity.

Jack also got a kick out of the Lord's usage of one of his oft-quoted expressions: "piece of cake." He was always touched by the fact that the Lord knows you inside out and expresses himself in jargon that is uniquely yours.

From that day on everything Jack did, although it was not always easy, he would give it extra effort until he had mastered it. Every day he literally takes the Lord by the hand and lifts the day up to him. The Lord reminded him that he truly is by his side every moment and he must rely on him only for strength. Jack remembered that he had always referred to the Lord as his constant companion, and told everyone how he was more real to him than flesh and blood.

"Not by might; nor by power, but by my spirit, saith the Lord of hosts"[61]

Pretty soon as he became more adept at everything, Jack's favourite expression became: "It's a piece of cake, if you know what you're doing," stressing that it doesn't just happen. You have to work at it with the Lord; then and only then does it become a "piece of cake." Sure enough, "Miracle Jack," who became "Fundamental Jack," now was dubbed "Piece-of-cake Jack!"

Jack started taking each day as his most precious possession. Not in the sense that this might be his last day and, therefore, live it to the fullest, but that he would live it to the best of his ability to the honour of his Lord. He has also been very mindful of not

---

[61] Zech. 4:6

142

turning back. As I had learned to do regarding all the negative images and thoughts trying to bombard me, he learned the meaning as never before of:

"..forgetting those things which are behind, and reaching forth unto those things which are before"[62]

Now he refuses to think back to the horrors behind him, most of which he does not remember, and is adamant about not wanting to know. Having been comatose, medicated, too sick to care, too weak and/or too confused for such a long time, he does not know many of the details of what happened then. When anyone brought it up, he would move out of the room, the thoughts of pain and hospital being still too fresh in his mind. Only recently since I started writing this book has he been able to deal gradually with the facts and to talk about them in a more detached way. He has confided that he doesn't know which side he would rather have been on, i.e. going through his trials or praying and watching, as he realizes neither was a "piece of cake." Once, he says, he did not know who he was, what he was, or where he was. But now he knows who he is, what he is and where he is! He refers to his right leg as "little Jack," and says that he did not get it back because he has not asked for it; it's not important to him!

Jack now only wants to concentrate on what his Lord has done for him and what he wants him to do for him. He has conversations with the Lord during the night where he "hears" the Lord talking to him. One night I overheard him, as if repeating something he had heard out loud: "But... where am I now?" He repeated it again, and then as if in answer: "I get it! I get it! Of course, you're not on the cross anymore; you have risen and are seated at the right hand of the Father![63] In other words, you do not look back on the suffering!"

We finally saw the neurologist on a Friday morning. The 2½-hour wait had totally exhausted Jack and he had slept most of the

---

[62] Phil. 3:13
[63] Heb. 10:12

afternoon. After supper he wanted to watch a video by another faith evangelist, a gift from our friend Jean. It is an anointed, descriptive teaching on healing, followed by hundreds of miracles happening all over the arena where he was ministering. We had watched it quite a number of times, but this time I knew that it was a divine appointment for Jack. I stayed quietly in the office, praying in the Spirit.

Just before the end Jack yelled to me: "Do you feel that anointing? Do you feel that anointing?" He wanted to be sure I heard him in the next room. I did; I had goosebumps all over me and went over to tell him so. It was time for bed and, as I leaned over to help him transfer to the wheelchair, he yelled out: "I'm healed!" He pounded his leg on the floor, saying: "See, I feel it; I feel it!" All the paralysis along his left side had totally and completely vanished!

Surprise? No! By now I could completely believe anything. I knew something was happening while Jack was watching that particular video at that precise time. I had felt it; I knew by the Holy Spirit just to be still and intercede separately. God, you are precious!

The anointing of God is on his Word. The Word preached under the anointing of the Holy Spirit, heartfelt praise and worship, coupled with a vibrant expectancy brings forth the glory of God. The Lord is present, even on the other side of a television screen! But, you must believe and expect your healing! Jesus is the Word made flesh. He is here! And he sure manifested himself again that evening!

"In the beginning was the Word, and the Word was with God, and the Word was God..."And the Word was made flesh, and dwelt among us..."[64]

Thank you, thank you, precious Lord!

The more his mental faculties improved, the more Jack's faith increased. He had always had a simple, childlike faith. Now his

[64] John 1:1;14

144

own faith, coupled with everyone else's and buoyed by all the teachings, was exploding as heavenly dynamite!

A month later we had a follow-up appointment with the neurologist. She asked Jack whether the medication had helped. Reaching in his pocket, he queried: "You mean these blue pills," triumphantly handing her the full bottle. She gasped and, before she could say anything, Jack looked her straight in the eye and said: "You see, doctor, the praises went up, the anointing came down, and I was completely healed!" Her mouth dropped open but nothing came out. Jack repeated it again. Right away she got up, checked Jack out, saw that he indeed had the full use of his left side, and said: "I guess I should send all my patients to him!" We answered in unison: "Absolutely!" With that she waved her hand, saying: "Get out of here!"

On our way home I said to Jack: "You know; it was not during the praise that this particular healing came about, referring to the vision and healing he had received in church." "Yeah, I know; but I was also praising the Lord while watching the video. Can you imagine the doctor believing that the anointing of God would come through a television screen?" We both laughed all the way home. The trip had been worthwhile just to see that doctor's face, and sow precious seeds into her life.

47. Everything In Place

The occupational therapist at our local C.L.S.C. had recommended a total alteration of our bathroom. It was very narrow and did not afford sufficient room for Jack to do his transfers from the wheelchair.

It took time to get the thought onto paper for recommendation and approval. A couple of months later an expert in the field came in to draw up a proposal which was then sent to the Quebec government for approval. At the same time an elevator was requested, which was to be installed onto the deck at the back of the house. This was exciting! I could wait no longer. My shoulders and upper back were constantly aching from pushing the wheelchair up the steep ramps.

All in all it took over a year before the approval was granted to cover financially part of the equipment and labour; subsequently the file was put on a waiting list. We had a new deck built that summer and waited patiently for the elevator. Jack had already been home a year and a half and, we found out, in summertime very little was done due to holidays. Time dragged on as our patience continued to be perfected.

In Montreal, frost generally arrives by mid October, and we were told that installation of the elevator would have to be postponed until the following spring. Oh no! I went on the prayer warpath again and, lo and behold, we had the most beautiful fall in Montreal history that year with absolutely no frost until the night of November 30th, when we were hit with a major snowstorm. That very day, which happened to be my birthday, the elevator was installed. What a perfect present! I could not imagine going through a whole winter again with those ramps, which by now were starting to fall apart. People everywhere were happily remarking about the wonderful autumn, and I would respond: "Thank the Lord! It is all because of Jack! I prayed for an elevator for him and voilà, we all got blessed!"

The bathroom did not get converted until February 2002. It took a whole month of tearing out and replacing walls; then the mess and dust, and later the painting and wallpapering! That February was one of the coldest on record with -40° C daytime temperatures, so we could not even open any windows. However, it was all worth it in the end. Now it is more than twice the size with ample room for wheelchair maneuvering and a wheel-in/walk-in shower; it's gorgeous! Thank-you, Lord!

The Lord sent a dear friend to lend both moral and tangible support to get me started on the painting, which initially seemed a totally insurmountable task. He even used Jack's orderly at the time. He was a capable, lighthearted and innovative young man, who would take Jack for a walk every morning when the weather was good. He loved gadgets and had just bought a revolutionary new vacuum as well as an electrostatic duster. He promptly brought them in the day after the workmen left and proceeded to dust most of the living room; he even left them for a couple of days for me to do the rest. Both appliances were marvelous; they actually turned what had seemed an impossible task into a game.

Jack's occupational therapist at the last rehabilitation centre suddenly replaced our current O.T. When she called to make an appointment, Jack was sitting on the deck. He told her that I had gone out for a walk, agreed that Thursday morning at 10 would be a good time for her to come, and that he was looking forward to seeing her again. When she came over, she was amazed at how well Jack was. She confessed that after hanging up the phone to make the appointment she had doubted whether Jack would remember to tell me about it, even though he sounded great! Remembering him from rehab with the short-term memory loss, she was totally in awe. She has since been very instrumental in lobbying the government for Jack to get his electric wheelchair.

One Saturday morning on short notice a young lady arrived from a community West of the city. When she got the phone call from the agency to replace the regular orderly, she told us that her initial reaction was that it would be ridiculous to go so far out of her territory. Then, as she looked down at the piece of paper on which she had scribbled Jack's name, she noticed the name was encircled in a bright light! She instantly knew that she had to accept this client. This gal was totally open to hear about what God had been doing in Jack's life. She gave her life to the Lord at our kitchen table, and went home with one of our faith tapes. Jack did not have to go out to share what the Lord had done; the Lord brought those whom he had selected right to our doorstep!

Sam, Jack's present orderly, is truly Jack's soul mate. The two of them talk non-stop, laugh all the time, go for walks, and challenge each other daily on local and world affairs. A few female caregivers were assigned from time to time. One asked Jesus to be Lord over her life, the other rededicated her life to him in our kitchen. They were both capable and warm. Everybody we dealt with in any phase of Jack's recuperation has heard about what the Lord has done. We pray that those seeds will take root in each and everyone's heart.

48. Our God Is an Awesome God!

No, the past 5½ years have not been the easiest. BUT GOD! Our awesome God was with us every step of the way. He was our peace that passes all human understanding, he raised Jack from the dead, and gave us the grace to forgive everyone who had made mistakes. He showed us that he is our healer.

A wise lawyer I was led to, who had previously been an I.C.U. head nurse, told me that doctors are but technicians. They are proud of their work; they do the best they can; but they cannot always find the glitch or fix the problem.

The most awesome lesson I have learned is that my Saviour is there every step of the way. He does not carry us in the sense that he does the work. No, like the mother eagle, he lets the fledgling fly and do its own thing while he hovers beneath so that when the little eaglet falters, he is there to catch it on his wings! And I faltered, over and over again. I have felt downhearted, physically exhausted, and unable to pray. There were times I felt that I could not stand in faith a moment longer, looking down at the circumstances over and over again. But he was always there to forgive, to sustain, to infuse with his strength, and to encourage. Furthermore, he always brought a person or happy circumstance my way when I most needed tangible support.

"My Lord and my God, I thank you, over and over again for everything you have done for all of us. I thank you most of all for prompting me to write Jack's testimony at this time. This is your appointed time as I was not able to do it before, nor would Jack have been helpful in supplying his insights as the emotional wounds had thus far been too tender. But, you knew that, dear Lord, and what a blessing it has been!"

"Holy Spirit, thank you for guiding my every word, and bringing to memory every detail and scripture with which you sustained me throughout the trials! It's in the looking back that I have really come to appreciate the awesome extent of how you have tenderly, yet firmly, held our family up every step of the way **with wings as eagles**! Your Name will be glorified, Lord, and our prayer is that every heart that reads this book will be touched by what you have done! Amen."

Appendix

The Bible tells us that Jesus Christ is the same yesterday, today and forever. He is unchanging and he is alive!

If you do not know him, Jack and I want to introduce you to our wonderful Saviour and Healer. We have shared a glimpse of him with you throughout this book but, if you, too, would like to know him personally as your Lord and Saviour, you're only a short prayer away! He is a gentleman; he will never impose himself on anyone. He has created us with a free choice to either accept or reject him.

According to the Word of God, we are all born in sin. Romans 3:10 says that:

"There is none righteous, no not one."

Jesus died on the cross in order to redeem us from sin. That means he paid the price to buy us back into the Kingdom of God! Wow! All we have to do is to acknowledge and thank him for his supreme sacrifice and to ask him to be Lord over our lives. We can then relinquish all the striving, sacrifices, and good works in order to try and hopefully be good enough to get into heaven. All our endeavours are like dirty rags to him. Titus 3:4-5 says it best:

"After that the kindness and love of God our Saviour toward man appeared, not by works of righteousness which we have done, but according to his mercy he saved us, by the washing of regeneration, and renewing of the Holy Ghost."

If you are ready to receive him now, just say this simple prayer out loud to him from your heart:

Dear Lord Jesus, I come to you as a little child. I repent of all my sins and shortcomings. I acknowledge that you died for me on that cross so long ago – even if I were the only person on the earth. I want to be born again and ask you to come into my heart and take control of my life. Thank you, Amen.

Congratulations and welcome to the family of God. If you have said this from the depth of your heart (and you will know that you know!), you are saved, or born again, as now your spirit is united with the Holy Spirit! Walk triumphantly hand in hand with the Lord in the newness of your life in the Holy Spirit!

Endnotes

---

i   Due to the stressful situation this continued until after Jack's return home, coinciding perfectly with early retirement!

ii   Now he reminds me regularly about that promise! He is back to being a waterfall of words, praise God!

iii   I cannot describe the look on her face when, on a walk with her dog, she saw Jack outside. She ran up and marvelled, acknowledging that she didn't think he would make it.

iv   We bumped into Sylvia, who lives in our neighbourhood, regularly. She has visited our home, and we keep in touch.

v   Recently I found out coincidentally (yeah sure!!) that they were neighbours of a dear sister in our church and that she has moved out West.

vi   Jack later told me that he distinctly heard a voice saying: "Now, get up!" very firmly. He knew that from that moment on he was healed, even though the physical manifestation did not happen until much later.

vii   Just before Jack was released from hospital, I bumped into her and was able to share about his miraculous healing.

viii   In May 2004, almost exactly 4 years after this last visit, Jack and I saw him again to ask him to sign authorization for access to the files to attest to all the medical facts stated above. He did. Jack shook his hand and thanked him for what he had done, and he acknowledged: "You know; I did not want to do it!" He was very surprised to see us and he felt visibly awkward regarding any mention that Jack's healing indeed was nothing less than miraculous.

ix   At the same time (May 2004) we tried to access this doctor as well, only to find out that he has moved to Texas.

Printed in the United States
107968LV00003B/109-150/A

9 781894 928465